ROSH HASHANAH YOM KIPPUR
SURVIVAL KIT

"The Survival Kit transforms what can be an uninspiring experience into a truly exhilirating one."

Rabbi Yaacov Weinberg - Baltimore
Rosh Yeshiva, Ner Israel Rabbinical College

"The Survival Kit is fun, meaningful, brilliantly written and totally engaging. If I had the resources I would buy a copy for every Jew in America."

Rabbi Ephraim Z. Buchwald - New York
Director, National Jewish Outreach Program
Rabbi, Lincoln Square Synagogue Beginners Service

ROSH HASHANAH
YOM KIPPUR
SURVIVAL KIT

by
Shimon Apisdorf

published by

LE*V*IATHAN PRESS

66 North Merkle Columbus, Ohio 43209
(614) 338-0774

Library of Congress Catalog Number: 92-81823

ISBN 1-881927-00-8

Thanks to Rabbi Meir Zlotowitz of Art Scroll Publications for permission to
reprint the story Dance of Suffering by Moshe Prager from *Sparks of Glory*.
Also, the story A Shofar in a Coffee Cauldron from *Hassidic Tales of the
Holocaust* © 1982 by Yaffa Eliach is reprinted by permission of Russell &
Volkening, Inc. as agents for the author. And, Rabbi Shlomo Baars for
questions in chapter five.

Photography (the forest, the trees, the author) by Miriam Apisdorf.
PRINTED IN THE UNITED STATES OF AMERICA

A LEVIATHAN PRESS PUBLICATION

The *Rosh Hashanah Yom Kippur Survival Kit* is available to
schools, synagogues and community organizations by special
order. See page 112.

ACKNOWLEDGEMENTS

Donna Cohen, Mark Barbour, Blair Axel, David Baum, Aron Blackman, Rick Cohen, Helen and Joe Berman, Kim McGarvey, Luis Kahn, Sharon Lessans, the Baker family, Aron Hoch, Shalom Schwartz, Mitch Mandel, Irving Stone, Shaya Pister, Shlomo Gogek and family, Shimon Weiner, Baruch Rabinowitz, Rabbi Mordechai and Chaya Blumenfeld, Earl & Sari Gorman, William Schottenstein, The Shores, The Jacobs, Rabbi Michel Twerski, Rabbi Shalom Shapiro, Rav Gil, Frank Nutis, Rabbi Alan G. Ciner, Rabbi Hirsh M. Chinn, Eric Schram, Wendy Walls, Jake Koval, Michael Monson, Rick Magder, Harvey and Sheila Hecker, Yaakov and Lori Palatnik, Avraham Leibowitz, Mike Berenstein, Dov Friedberg, Barry and Rita and the kids, Yehudis Silverstein, Joseph Frasco, Yitzchak Greenman, Mitchel Shore Creative Services, Killer, Pal and Zale Newman.

APPRECIATION

Ann Apisdorf, sister, friend, student and confidant. Asher Resnick, a friend. Michael (you're all heart) Hart. Yossi and Judy Abrams, one in a million. Yechezkal Mordechai (Albert) Nemani, a teacher. Reuven, Reuben, Robin, Rubeno Nemani— call collect please! Mrs. Pauline Eisenmann, a good neighbor. Russell ("the Saver") Simmons, a mensch personified. Harry Apisdorf, what a brother is supposed to be. Aish HaTorah, my teachers and friends. Rabbi Noah Weinberg, Rosh Hayeshiva and source of inspiration.

SPECIAL THANKS

My parents David and Bernice Apisdorf who possess the courage to allow their children to chart their own course all the while building a close and loving family.

Mr. and Mrs. Robert and Charlotte Rothenburg, whose love and kindness know no bounds.

Esther Rivka, Ditzah Leah and Yitzchak Ben Zion. It is a privilege to have such children.

My wife, my blessing, my source of goodness. Miriam. A woman of valor whose love, dedication and hands-on involvement have shaped every page of this book as she does every day of our life together.

Hakadosh Baruch Hu, source of all blessing.

...for the surface of Moses' face shone...

Dedicated
to the memory of

Manfred E. Hart

who, like Moses,
in a humble, passionate way,
abidingly brightened this world
and all those whom he touched.

CONTENTS

1

INTRODUCTION

So Much to Do, So Little Time

A few years ago a Canadian radio station aired a documentary series which looked at early twentieth century inventions that were touted as products that would *"change your life."* There is no doubt that the last 100 years are replete with products and inventions that have indeed altered the way we live. It's hard to imagine what life would be like without disposable plastic wraps, containers and bottles — can you believe that milk once came in a bottle! From telephones to copy machines and then to the fax — who knows what's next? — maybe *"beam me up, Scotty"* is just around the corner.

There is one image from that documentary which still stays with me — the piece about early advertisements for the first sewing machines. It seemed that the assumption underlying the content and tone of those ads was, *what will women do with all the free time they will now have on their hands?* It was clear that the sewing machine would usher in an era of leisure totally unprecedented in the history of mankind.

The irony, of course, is that with the plethora of devices and services designed to save us time and increase our efficiency we seem to have less time and be more harried than ever before. It's a Catch-22, of sorts. The more time I have, the more I can do, and the more I can do, the more time I need. Hence, we try to fill every hour saved by our PC with two hours of other work or fun (mostly work), thus pushing us to discover ways to create another additional hour of time to accommodate the increased load. This deadly cycle soon spawns a new generation of time-saving inventions which are again followed by more activities to fill the new empty spaces. The end result is that what once took a week now takes a day and what once took a month or more is now only a week's work.

Are you still puzzled at the fact that we are a society running on empty? We are forever burning ourselves out trying to compress year's worth of activities into just one twelve-month slot. Eventually, something has to give.

Judaism: Caught in the Squeeze

There exists today an intense competition over who and what will fill the ever-shrinking discretionary time in our schedules. Where once Judaism was printed in strong, bold letters across our calendars, today it is lucky to get *"penciled in"* for even a few days in the entire year.

If Judaism were a corporation, I would assert that it has done a miserable job of marketing itself to the educated, discerning consumer of the last half of the twentieth century. It is my contention, however, that the issue is one of marketing and not one of product quality. This doesn't mean that Judaism should suddenly take to the airwaves with some slick Madison Avenue ad campaign (although it's a thought), but rather that we should look at the medium through which the message of Judaism has been communicated these last decades and see if we can't understand the problems and offer a solution.

Just Do It and Don't Ask Questions

The dominant medium for communicating Judaism to this generation has been the synagogue or community Hebrew schools. Whatever Jewish education most people possess today came from those after-school or Sunday morning classes which we all swore we would never subject our children to. Another medium was our parents or grandparents. While no one can dispute that their hearts were deeply rooted in the right place, the fact remains that even the deepest of sentiments in no way readied them for the task of articulating Jewish values in a relevant and cogent manner. More often than not, their fall back position was — *"we do it because we're Jewish and that's just the way it is."* And for better or worse, such an argument no longer carries the weight it once did.

Dennis Prager puts it this way: "Jews may know how to survive but they do not know why to survive . . . Jewish life concentrates on *how* to rescue persecuted Jews, *how* to gain political support for Israel . . . Religious Jewish life, too, generally ignores the *why* and focuses almost exclusively on the *how*." The problem with Jewish education has been that we have stressed the mechanics of Judaism — the **what** and the **how** — and have neglected the **why**. In a world where people carefully consider which activities will fill their time, you had better give them a darn good reason for choosing High Holiday services over the World Series, or quite frankly — you don't stand a chance! Of course, there is always good old-fashioned Jewish guilt, but wouldn't it be tragic if the people of the book, the people of monotheism, Maimonides, and *"Nation shall not lift up sword against nation"* should be left with nothing to appeal to other than the specter of callously rubbing the tender feelings of an aging parent or grandparent.

The *Why* of Being Jewish

The *Rosh Hashanah Yom Kippur Survival Kit* is just the tip of an iceberg. Its purpose is to demonstrate that Judaism has nothing to be ashamed of when it comes to the superior quality of its intellectual and spiritual content. The Survival Kit assumes that if people were to possess a mature understanding of what Judaism has to say to our lives today, then it would easily hold its own in the fiercely competitive environment in which we live.

As I alluded to earlier, every aspect of Jewish life consists of three primary components. These are **what**, **how** and **why**. Let's take Passover as an example. **What** do you do on Passover — you make a seder. **How** do you make a seder — you get a box or two of matzo, some wine, a few Maxwell House haggadahs — you shlepp your family to the table — and presto, a seder! Then comes the issue of **why**. Why do we do all these things at seder. Why four cups of wine and not five, why do we recline and so on.

Isn't it obvious that if we never meaningfully address the question of **why**, then eventually our Judaism will become a hollow sentimental ritual at best, a dreary burden at worst. In Jewish law it is considered torture to have someone perform a purposeless task. To carry out a mindless function with no comprehension of the purpose it fulfills is fine if you are dealing with automatons. For Jews, as for all people, it is ultimately debasing and inspires either total lethargy or violent revolution. The Jewish community today is confronted with both of these on a massive scale.

The *Rosh Hashanah Yom Kippur Survival Kit* is a partial attempt to address the issue of **why** within the context of the High Holiday services. If the statistics are correct, most Jews today no longer have any synagogue affiliation whatsoever. I would be surprised if more than fifty percent of Jews in America attend Rosh Hashanah and Yom Kippur services anymore. I would be even more surprised if more than twenty percent of those who do attend don't start looking for the exit shortly after their arrival. How can a day in synagogue possibly be meaningful or inspiring if you don't understand the meaning behind the prayers you are reciting or the conceptual basis on which the holiday is based?

This book has been written for three types of people. Firstly, it is for people who are not planning to attend synagogue this year. It will give you a radically different understanding of Rosh Hashanah and Yom Kippur and perhaps your entire Jewish identity. Likewise, if you are planning to attend services but are dreading the experience, then again — this book has been written for you. What's more, I would suggest you read it twice. Once during the weeks before Rosh Hashanah and again during the services themselves. Lastly, if you are amongst those who already have some sense of the meaning of these holidays, then I think that you — perhaps more than anyone else — will find the Survival Kit to be a worthwhile intellectual and spiritual supplement to your experience in synagogue this year.

Wishing you a Shana Tova, a sweet new year.

Shimon Apisdorf

2

PROLOGUE: WHAT'S A HOLIDAY?

Two Views of Time

Classically there are two models for viewing time, one linear and one cyclical. The linear view imagines time to be an infinitely long line with three component parts — past, present, and future. Today we stand in the present and if we but peer over our shoulder we will behold a long line of time stretching back deeper and deeper into the murky realm of the past. The future is simply the continuation of this same line waiting to progress endlessly ahead of us.

The cyclical notion of time conjures up a different image. In this model we keep going around and around in circles forever wearing a deeper rut in the same track. With specific regard to the Jewish holidays our concept of time more resembles the cyclical view — though not in its strictest sense — than the linear.

Holidays as Seasons

If you live in a climate that exhibits few significant seasonal changes then you are missing out on one of life's most delightful experiences. There is nothing more enchanting than the buds of springtime working their magic to restore our trees to life; the first morning when you open your window and hear the birds singing;

the variegated leaves of autumn; or a silent snowfall.

In a society that moves from home to car to office and back again — each with its own background music — we barely feel the impact of the shifts in seasons. The pace is too fast. The music too loud. The loss, well, incalculable.

If, however, you make the effort to take an occasional walk and feel the moods of the seasons then your life is so much the richer. But beyond the sheer beauty you also know that each season has a distinct feel. A resonance that your psyche responds to. There *is* something special in the air in springtime. And yes, in the fall it's there too, all together different, but no less enchanting.

So too the holidays. More than once the annual cycle of the Jewish year has been dubbed "seasons of the soul." Each spring we pack away our layers of sweaters and dust the winter's dormancy off our bicycle seats. We're free again. Just like we were last spring, only not quite.

Each year Passover comes. We pack away the bread products and dust off those grape juice–stained haggadahs. In Hebrew, Passover is labeled *Z'man Heruteynu* — the time of our freedom. We're free again. Just like we were last Passover, only not quite.

Seasons As Opportunities

Every holiday has its own personality. Its own feel. There is a singular opportunity for personal growth that exists within the observance of each holiday that is present at no other time during the year.

Passover is called *the time of our freedom* because at that time you can comprehend and actualize personal freedom in a way that cannot be achieved at any other time during the year. It's in the air, ripe for the picking. So too the festival of Succos which bears the title — *the time of our joy*. If you want to understand what joy is and successfully deal with the inner conflicts that inhibit its expression, then you've got to live in a succah for a week. On Succos the door to the candy store has been left wide open.

Whoever wants can come in and help themselves. Joy is an idea, a state of mind and a challenge. Joy is a tool for living, and on Succos it's there to be better understood and more fully integrated into the fabric of your being.

Rosh Hashanah and Yom Kippur

If you've been to Paris but you missed the Louvre then you haven't been to Paris. If you participate in a Jewish holiday and you're not different as a result, if you haven't grown, then you missed the whole point of the holiday.

Rosh Hashanah and Yom Kippur, like all Jewish holidays, are enormous opportunities for personal growth. There is almost no limit to what you can achieve on these days.

It is no wonder that the month of Elul, the month before Rosh Hashanah, is viewed as a month of preparation for the days of Rosh Hashanah and Yom Kippur. The quality of any trip will in large part be a reflection of the preparation put in ahead of time. So too the High Holidays, these days of awe — of awesome opportunity — for insight and growth.

This is the purpose of the *Rosh Hashanah Yom Kippur Survival Kit*. It has been written to give you some appreciation of what can be accomplished on these days. Admittedly it only begins to scratch the surface. But you must know — even this surface is so fertile, so rich in possibilities for growing, for becoming a more fully developed human being and Jew   that years can be spent harvesting the bounty of this spiritual topsoil. Beneath it lie riches beyond our wildest dreams.

Rosh Hashanah and Yom Kippur are a personal odyssey. The *machzor* — the High Holiday prayer book — serves as the primary guide for this odyssey and yet in its extensive detail only outlines the most important landmarks. Along the way we find that each one of these landmarks resides within each and every one of us. They come in the form of questions that ask us what we want to achieve with our lives. Or, as statements of values that give us cause to stop and reflect. To rethink our innerlives and the implications of the choices we have made.

Each prayer, each internal landmark, calls us away from the stagnation that the routine of life breeds and urges us to reassert our determination that life will always be an exciting quest for understanding and personal development.

The less children seem to grow and develop, the less attention we adults seem to pay them. For mature, sensitive, thinking adults, Rosh Hashanah and Yom Kippur contain the tools that will help ensure that our lives continue to grow and develop long after our shoe sizes reach their outer limits.

A Word about Judaism

Judaism makes demands. If it is anything, it is anything but a religion of comfort. *The Shulchan Aruch* (the code for Jewish living) opens with the statement that *"in the morning a person should rise with the vitality of a lion."*

Let's be honest. When was the last time you felt like a lion in the morning — ready to attack the new day with every ounce of vitality you possessed.

How precious they are, so rarified, those moments when we feel that there is nothing we would rather do than confront life and its challenges head-on. More likely, if you're like most of us, your first impulse upon awakening in the morning is to hit that beloved snooze button and roll over for another twenty minutes of dream-filled bliss.

Together, Rosh Hashanah and Yom Kippur are the dawning moments of a new year. They are 365 mornings all rolled into three days of directed energy. If you feel like rolling over and going back to sleep (after all, you've been through these holidays before), I beg of you, don't. These three days, like Judaism and Jewish life itself, call us to transcend our first inclinations and to strive for a greatness we so long to achieve but are so hesitant to pursue. Rosh Hashanah and Yom Kippur, like life, will take a great deal of effort, perhaps even some pain.

But isn't that what you will teach your children? That the pursuit of comfort is the antithesis of the search for excellence. That if you want to achieve anything of enduring value in life that it will take great determination and effort.

Do your ears hear what your lips speak? The truth about life is so very plain. The challenges — and the rewards — so incredibly enormous. If only we could get out of bed.

Here then is the *Rosh Hashanah Yom Kippur Survival Kit*. Its aim is far more than its title — survival. It is my hope that with the help of this book you will not only survive your experience in synagogue this year but that you will emerge from the holidays with a new appreciation for the thrilling challenge we call life.

ROSH HASHANAH

The Forest

3

SURVIVAL KIT USER'S GUIDE

The *Rosh Hashanah Yom Kippur Survival Kit* has been designed to help make these holidays — their prayers, themes, and symbols come alive for you. Here are a few suggestions that will help you get the most out of the kit.

1) Sometime before the holidays —

A) Leaf through the material and familiarize yourself with the contents.

B) During the month before Rosh Hashanah read the essays in chapters 8, 10, 12, 15, 16, and 18. These essays explain many primary intellectual and spiritual concepts which will help you develop a personalized perspective and approach to the holidays.

C) These essays — or any part of the Survival Kit — can be read together with family or friends. In past years people have used the book as a focal point for informal study groups and have found that the discussion generated in these groups has led to a deeper appreciation of the holidays and their inherent potential.

D) Take a look at your *machzor* (High Holiday prayer book) and put an asterisk(*) on the pages where there are corresponding comments in the Survival Kit. This will allow you to use your machzor and this book in an integrated fashion.

2) Take the Survival Kit with you to synagogue —

A) The Survival Kit is not a prayer book and is not meant to take the place of your machzor; rather it is a supplementary guide that can be used in various ways.

    i. Where this kit comments on a prayer, read the comments prior to saying the prayer. The comments are designed to help focus your thoughts on one or two themes within a particular prayer.

    ii. If the formality of the service gets to be a bit much you can change pace by reading one of the essays in the kit.

B) Synagogue is a place for reflection as well as prayer. Some of the questions, issues, and ideas covered in the Survival Kit can serve as useful guideposts for meaningful introspection.

4

HOW TO SURVIVE SYNAGOGUE

" . . . but Rabbi, even if I can read some of the prayers I still don't understand what I'm saying . . . To tell you the truth I'd rather take a quiet reflective walk in the park this year than spend all that time in synagogue saying a bunch of words that don't really mean so much to me anyway . . ."

Prayer is meant to be a powerful, relevant and meaningful experience. Here are a few ideas to keep in mind this year that should help to make the services as personally uplifting as possible.

1)   Five minutes of prayer said with understanding, feeling, and a personal connection to the words and their significance means far more than five hours of lip service.

2)   "Unfulfilled expectations lead to self-imposed frustrations." Therefore, don't expect to be "moved" by every prayer or to follow along with the entire service.

3)   Read through the prayers and slowly think about what you're saying and don't be overly concerned about being behind. Look, the worst that could happen is that you will fall behind, but don't worry, they'll probably announce the

pages so you can always catch up.

4) If a particular sentence or paragraph touches you — linger a while. Say the words over and over to yourself. Softly but audible to your ear. Allow those words to touch you. Feel them. And, if you're really brave, then close your eyes and say those words over and over for a couple of moments.

5) You're not that proficient in Hebrew? Don't worry, G-d understands whatever language you speak. And, like a loving parent, *He* can discern what's in your heart even if you can't quite express it the way you would like.

6) As you sit in your synagogue on Rosh Hashanah and Yom Kippur you are joined by millions of Jews in synagogues all over the world. You are a Jew and you are making a powerful statement about your commitment to Judaism and the Jewish people.

5

"ASK A JEW A QUESTION . . ."

Holidays in Jewish thought are far more than commemorations of past events. Rosh Hashanah is certainly more than a Jewish January 1st.

The essential opportunity of Rosh Hashanah is to clarify for ourselves what our truest, "bottom line" priorities are in life. No time is more appropriate than today for asking ourselves some basic questions in order to clarify — and remind ourselves — what it is that is truly important to us and who it is we ultimately want to be.

To reflect on some of the following questions is quite apropos on this, the day of judgment.

1)   When do I most feel that my life is meaningful?

2)   Those who mean the most to me — have I ever told them how I feel?

3)   Are there any ideals I would be willing to die for?

4)   If I could live my life over, would I change anything?

5)   What would bring me more happiness than anything else in the world?

6)   What are my three most significant achievements since last Rosh Hashanah?

7)   What are the three biggest mistakes I've made since last Rosh Hashanah?

8)   What project or goal, if left undone, will I most regret next Rosh Hashanah?

9)   If I knew I couldn't fail — what would I undertake to accomplish in life?

10)   What are my three major goals in life?
       — What am I doing to achieve them?
       — What practical steps can I take in the next two months towards these goals?

11)   If I could only give my children three pieces of advice what would they be?

These questions can also be used at your family meals to create great conversation. Try going around the table and asking everyone to respond to one of the questions.

6

SEVEN QUESTIONS PEOPLE ASK ABOUT ROSH HASHANAH

(I)

Question: Why don't we celebrate New Year's in January?

Answer: The calendar which begins in January and ends in December is known as the Gregorian calendar and was introduced by Pope Gregory XIII in 1582. This calendar is based on an even earlier calendar — the Julian calendar — which was introduced by Julius Caesar in 46 B.C.

The Jewish calendar is not only of much earlier origin, but differs from the Gregorian calendar in numerous ways.

1)   The Jewish calendar is based on the moon (lunar) and not the sun (solar).

2)   The Jewish calendar contains a number of "new year" dates. This is like having a fiscal year that overlaps two calendar years. The month of Tishrei, which begins with Rosh Hashanah, is the beginning of the year vis-à-vis the number of years, i.e., 5752, 5753, etc. The month of Nissan, the month in which Passover falls, is considered the beginning of the year with regard to the festivals (Passover, Shavuos and Succos) as well as for the establishment of the reign of a Jewish king.

Insights: Our calendar is based on the moon, and, similarly the Jewish people are compared to the moon. No sooner has the moon disappeared into utter darkness than the first illuminated sliver reappears. No matter how dark things seem for the Jewish people, we must know that the "light" is already waiting to reappear. Jewish history is an ongoing portrayal of this principle. Also, unlike the sun which is always present in its fullest form, the moon progresses in stages until it is full and radiant. A Jew must look at life as a constant process of growth and development. Tiny beginnings can grow to their fullest potential and even darkness can be overcome.

(II)

Question: On Chanukah the menorah burned for eight days; on Passover the Jews left Egypt — what happened on Rosh Hashanah?

Answer: The Talmud relates that man was created on the first of Tishrei. This being the case, Rosh Hashanah is a birthday of sorts for the human race.

Insights: The account of the creation of man in the Torah states that man was created *"in the image of G-d."* The meaning of this is that man possesses free will. Our actions are not predetermined by any divine, psychological, or sociological forces; rather we are free to choose and are thus responsible for the consequences of our actions. As will be explained later, on Rosh Hashanah we celebrate our humanity by exercising our free will.

(III)

Question: Is Rosh Hashanah a happy day or a sad day?

Answer: Rosh Hashanah is a happy day, a festival, and at the same time it is a very serious day. It is a serious day because it is the day of judgment and it is a happy day because we are confident that if we understand the meaning of the day and use it properly, then we will indeed prevail with a favorable judgment.

(IV)

Question: Why does G-d judge us?

Answer: Because life is serious business. If we feel that we are being judged, we are more apt to treat life with the proper gravity.

Insights: Big G-d cares about little me. Judgment implies caring. If you don't care you don't judge. Therefore, another way of understanding how Rosh Hashanah is both solemn and joyous is that we look at G-d's judgment, the fact that He cares about how we live our lives, as the surest sign of His love.

(V)

Question: Why do we dip an apple in honey?

Answer: It tastes good! Also, because it represents our heartfelt wishes for a sweet year, not only for ourselves and our families but for all the Jewish people.

Insights: (1) On most fruit trees the leaves appear before the fruit, thus providing a protective cover for the young fruit. The apple, however, makes a preemptive move by appearing before the leaves. The Jewish people are compared to an apple because we are willing to live out our Jewish lives even if this seems to leave us unprotected. We have confidence that G-d and the instructions in the Torah could never mislead us. (2) A bee can inflict pain by its sting, yet it also produces delicious honey. Life has the same duality of potential. We pray that our choices will result in a sweet year.

(VI)

Question: Why do we blow the Shofar?

Answer: Since Rosh Hashanah is the anniversary of the creation of the world it follows that it is also the anniversary of G-d being sovereign over the world. Rosh Hashanah is a coronation of sorts and thus we trumpet the shofar just like at a coronation ceremony.

(VII)

Question: If you don't have a shofar will a trumpet or some other instrument suffice?

Answer: No. Our sages teach us that it is specifically a ram's horn that must be used. This is an allusion to the binding of Isaac which took place on Rosh Hashanah, where a ram eventually replaced Isaac on the altar.

Insights: Abraham and Isaac, each in his own way, were prepared to give up everything for what they believed was right — the will of their creator. When we hear the sound of the ram's horn on Rosh Hashanah we are supposed to consider what sacrifices we would make for what we believe in as Jews.

- If things looked dire — would we go fight for Israel?
- Would we pass up a good job opportunity if it meant living in a place where our children's Jewish education would be compromised?
- Would we give up a month's pay if it were required to help resettle Soviet Jews in Israel?

7

HIGHLIGHTS OF THE ROSH HASHANAH MORNING SERVICE

Birchas HaShachar / Morning Blessings

Asher Yatzar / Who Has Designed Man with Wisdom

If you gently push the side of one of your eyes you will see two images begin to separate. Your eyes actually see two different images at slightly different angles; it's your brain that blends the two, thereby creating one three-dimensional image. This image is projected onto the retina at the back of your eye. As your gaze shifts from object to object at varying distances, your lens automatically adjusts the focus to keep the picture crystal clear. Your retina consists of hundreds of millions of cells that convert these images into electrical impulses. These impulses are then relayed to your brain (without the use of a modem), which in turn "reads" the impulses and tells you that the image which created this pattern of impulses is in fact a flower.

Nikon — move over.

In this prayer we focus on the wonder of our bodily functions. The complexity and fragility are equally humbling.

Birchas HaTorah / Blessings for the Torah

The Torah — instructions for living. Wisdom, moral teachings, and commandments. Insight, guidelines, and guidance.

The Jewish people have been scattered. We speak various languages and come in a variety of sizes and colors. We have different opinions, different practices and an endless collage of customs.

All that we have in common is the Torah. It is what binds us with each other today and with the Jews of decades and centuries gone by. The more we probe the Torah for life's insights, the more we study — and study together — the closer we will become. In these blessings we thank G-d for commanding us to be involved in the study of Torah.

Aylu Devarim / These Matters Have No Set Measure

On the night of the Passover seder there is a *mitzva* (a commandment) to eat matzo. But a nibble won't do — there is a minimum prescribed amount which must be eaten. Similarly, many other observances are limited to specific "measures," specific amounts.

This is not so, however, when it comes to acts of human compassion and kindness or to developing a relationship with G-d or pursuing the wisdom stored in our Torah.

For these life defining essentials we must use our own best judgment. For those elements which determine the tone of our life's involvements we are the final arbiters of priority. How highly this speaks of our ability and integrity. How weighty this renders our responsibility.

Elokai Neshama / **The Soul**

Save the whales, save the spotted owl, or save a human being. Which one takes precedence? Are any of these lives more valuable than the others?

Consider this: if the essential difference between a man and an animal lies in the realm of intelligence, then is human life any more valuable than animal life just because we happen to be smarter?

At this point in the morning service we focus on the fact that there is something else, another part of us that separates us from our pets. It is that part of us that stands in awe, transfixed by a brilliant sunset or by the waves coming to shore in the dead of night.

Brochos / **Morning Blessings**

Never have so many wanted so much and found so little.

Happiness, the true treasure of living. "Who is wealthy?" our sages asked. "He who takes pleasure in what he has."

Our eyes and our ears. Our friends and our family. Our homes, our cars, our health and yes, even our ability to get out of bed in the morning and stand on our own two feet.

The prayerbook reminds us — be thankful for *all* we have.

Shachris / **The Morning Service**

HaMelech / **The King**

On Rosh Hashanah we proclaim G-d as king. Our sovereign ruler as well as our judge.

A child does not have to be beaten to be abused. To ignore a child so that he feels you don't care and you're not interested is the worst abuse. Such a child would rather be yelled at — even punished — than ignored.

The day of judgment means that G-d is interested in us. He cares. What we do *does* ultimately matter.

The Shema / **Hear O Israel**

Sartre's first major work was entitled *Nausea*. Because that is what one must feel if one stares an accidental and meaningless existence in the face.

Shema Yisroel! A Jew lives to teach the world that there is a G-d. That our existence is not an odd fluke, and that life is a precious and meaningful opportunity.

Amidah / **The Standing Prayer**

The *Amidah* is commonly referred to as the silent prayer. This, however, is a misnomer, for the *Amidah* is to be said softly, not silently, to yourself. The words should be audible to your ears and your ears alone. To your heart and your heart alone.

Far too often the Jewish people have been faced with despair. But, rather than wither we have responded with hope, with courage, and even with joy and optimism.

Much of the *Amidah* is an expression of our longing for a better, more humane world.

Hashem Sefasai Tiftach / **G-d Open My Lips**

A toddler thinks that she cannot walk, but she can. A child fears he will never swim, but he will. Many of our limitations in life are more perceived than real. It is only ghosts which are holding us back.

In Hebrew the word for lips is the same as the word for *banks*, as in *river banks*. The banks of a river define its limitations. When we say "G-d, open my lips," we are also saying, "G-d, help me to see beyond my perceived limitations."

Man: Microcosm of the Universe

G-d created two worlds. One of immense proportions and another equally vast though not manifestly so.

In Hebrew the word for world, or universe, is *olam*. The universe is referred to as *olam hagadol*, the macro-universe. Man is known to our sages as *olam hakatan*, the micro-universe. The word *olam* also has another connotation: it means concealment. The fullness of what is contained in an olam, a world, is not always apparent.

Man, microcosm of the universe that he is, is the keeper of a potential that borders on the infinite. On one level this defies our comprehension, while in the same instance it is plainly so. We all wonder if there is anything that lies beyond the reach of man.

Each and everyone of us. One minute you see it and the next it seems to vanish. Our potential. It stretches as far as the eye can see.

Zachrenu L'Chaim / Remember Us for Life

The voice was that of one who survived the unfathomable hell of Auschwitz. A silent terror still lines his face   even when he smiles.

"If I had a choice," he said, "of having to relive every torturous moment again — or — to be a German guard in the camps, I'd go through it all again rather than serve for even one hour as a guard."

The guards lived and breathed. They went home to wives and children — they enjoyed the finest classical music and they laughed — all in a day's work. But they were dead.

The life that we ask for and strive for on Rosh Hashanah is more than just survival. It's a life of value and meaning. You can be alive and dead or you can be alive and live. Choose life!

Magen Avraham / Shield of Abraham

There is, they say, a little bit of Abraham in all of us. Abraham, founder of the Jewish nation, was one man in a very foreign world. No one — literally no one — thought the way he did. No one shared his values, his vision, his dedication to meaningful actions.

"I" am the fusion of body and soul, physical and spiritual. At times it seems the soul is so alone, forever lost in the fatty recesses of the body, in the murky world of materialism.

In Yiddish it's known as the *pintele yid*. There is a part of every Jew, a longing that can never be extinguished. A bit of light, no matter how dim, forever shines.

The miracle of the exodus of Russian Jews to Israel is not so much that they are finally free, not so much that there even exists an Israel to receive them, but that by the thousands and hundreds of thousands they still care very much about being Jewish. Seventy years of relentless physical and psychological oppression was unable to extinguish the Abraham — that spark in the Jewish soul.

An Israeli newspaper reported that tens of thousands of recent Russian immigrants, children and adults, have received a bris mila (circumcision) upon their arrival in Israel. Many of these take place in almost assembly line fashion with the mohel performing one after another. A newspaper reporter was questioning the immigrants waiting in line about the motivation for their actions. When asked if he believed in G-d, one middle-aged Russian who was raised on a steady diet of Communist propaganda declared, "No, I don't believe in G-d, I'm an atheist." The curious reporter, a bit taken aback, went on, "Then why are you having a bris?" There in the land of Israel, the land of King David and the Maccabees, of the Western Wall and Ethiopian Jews, the Russian answered proudly, "Without a bris, it is impossible to be a Jew!"

Only a Jewish atheist could utter such words, and only the spark of Abraham could yield such an atheist.

U'Vchayn Tayn Pach'dcha / Instill Awe and Fear

Did you ever notice how people will pay good money to be frightened? Millions of people visit amusement parks each year. And where do you find the longest lines — the roller coaster. That ride which tries to convince you that your next moment will be your last.

A brush with death is exhilarating. If you've ever had a "close call" in a car then you know that you were far more alert and alive after the narrow escape than you were the entire day before.

In Hebrew the word for fear is "yira," which means to see or to perceive. If you choose to see life for what it is, an enormous opportunity and a serious responsibility, rather than look the other way, well — that can be frightening, or, exhilarating.

U'Vchayn Tzadikim / The Righteous Will See and Be Glad

Far too often the Jewish people have come face to face with utter despair. Surely history would pardon us if we succumbed to lethargy in the face of this relentless confrontation.

But we have chosen otherwise. We have responded with optimism and hope even where there seemed to be none. With quiet courage and with joy. You read the newspapers, day in and day out, and you long for a more humane world. We believe in it — despite the headlines.

Avinu Malkeinu / Our Father Our King

A father has a very special love for each and every one of his children, but not necessarily the means to give them everything he wants.

An omnipotent king looks out from his palace and sees a nation, faceless individuals he will never know.

Avinu Malkeinu, a high-tech war in the Persian Gulf brings down a shower of missiles on a largely undefended Israel. In such a scenario, the pundits predicted, hundreds if not thousands would be lost.

Avinu Malkeinu, hundreds of buildings were reduced to rubble and yet there was scarcely a casualty.

8

MORNING TORAH READINGS

An Overview

The Phenomenon of Jewish Survival (First Day Reading)

How is it that the Jewish people have survived — and why? The greatest of minds, historians and philosophers alike, are humbled as they grope for an answer to this enigma of human history.

On the first day of Rosh Hashanah we read about the birth of a son named Isaac to an elderly couple named Abraham and Sarah. A pattern was established for Jewish history. Given the advanced ages of Abraham and Sarah, an Isaac should never have been born, but he was. Given the forces at work against Jewish survival, we simply should not be here, but we are.

The Meaning of Jewish Survival (Second Day Reading)

The purpose of Jewish survival does not lie in some deep-seated desire to be listed in the *Guinness Book of World Records* under the heading, "Longest History for a Persecuted People." Rather, the purpose and meaning of our history is to make a difference. To have an impact on how mankind looks at itself and the world it inhabits.

In the midst of civilizations that glorified the warrior and the wars he fought, the prophet Isaiah gave voice to the revolutionary Jewish idea, *"Nation shall not lift up sword against nation, neither shall they learn war anymore."*

Today, two millennia later, these same words are etched on the facade of the United Nations headquarters. Ask yourself which is more inexplicable: the dogged persistence of this notion in the face of a hostile world, or the survival of the people that carried this message in that same oppressive milieu.

It's absolutely breathtaking. A depth of commitment that was able to transcend any obstacle, to defy all odds. The events recorded in the second day Torah reading set the stage for this, our ultimate commitment.

The Big Bang Theory of Rosh Hashanah: An Essay

When was the last time you experienced judgment day? Was it when your boss said to you, *"Can you come into my office before you leave today? I'd like to speak with you."* Or, perhaps, you had a court date. A real-life experience of sitting before a judge, being examined and cross-examined, and having to answer for your actions, thoughts, and intentions.

How about in your own mind. You were lying awake one night or driving along in a car without the radio on. When you were the court. Everything wrapped up in one mind, one conscience. Judge, jury, prosecutor and defendant.

We have all lived through days of judgment. Days when the past has come back to haunt us.

In the Torah portion for the first day of Rosh Hashanah we find the following statement. *"And G-d heard the voice of the young boy, and then an angel of G-d called to Hagar from heaven and said to her, what is the matter with you Hagar? Do not be afraid, for G-d has heard the voice of the young boy right where he is."*

When the sages of the Talmud refract this verse through the unique lens of wisdom that is theirs, a mystifying perspective on

Rosh Hashanah comes to the fore.

This *"young boy"* was Yishmael, Abraham's son. Even as a young boy, Yishmael was a cold-blooded murderer. As an adult, he and his descendants would grow to be bitter oppressors of the Jewish people.

Yishmael lay there abandoned, left to die. But G-d caused Hagar to notice a well and she was able to draw water and save the life of Yishmael. Why, Why! That Yishmael had an evil past was well known, that his future would sow seeds of even greater evil and destruction — this was known to G-d.

At that moment, *"right where he is,"* Yishmael was being judged. Our sages tell us that the dynamics of judgment as they applied to Yishmael apply to us too. On Rosh Hashanah G-d looks at us *right where we are.* At first blush our sages have given us good reason to breathe a sigh of relief. Think about it. Right where you are! G-d, though He knows the future, will not take it into account. Fair enough. But listen to this — G-d won't even take our past into account. All we have to do is get our act together for one day. Say what we are supposed to say, do what we are supposed to do, act the way we are supposed to act and don't worry. The future doesn't count, the past is irrelevant, we will only be judged according to who we are on the day of Rosh Hashanah itself.

Sages or no sages, that doesn't seem to make sense. Or for that matter, to be just or right.

We are being asked to pause. To think for a moment and to take a second look at the meaning of Rosh Hashanah as the day of judgment.

So let us do just that. Let us take a second and deeper look at Rosh Hashanah, at judgment and at ourselves.

Current theory regarding the nature of the origin of the universe is commonly referred to as the Big Bang Theory. This theory posits that before the big bang occurred, there was no time, space, matter, or energy. What was there, you may ask? Obviously there was nothing. Well, if there was nothing — how does nothing "explode" in a big bang and become a universe?

What preceded the big bang was an infinitesimally small mathematical point which was not made up of matter, contained no energy, occupied no space, and preceded time itself. Paradoxically, this inconceivably tiny point contained within it the entire universe. This tiny, primordial point represents ultimate potential. Whatever it was, when it "exploded" it unleashed an entire universe. From gravity to time and from protons to cockroaches it was all present in some form before the big bang took place.

Rosh Hashanah is the big bang. On Rosh Hashanah we neither ponder our future nor grapple with our past. On Rosh Hashanah we confront our ultimate potential.

Each one of us is destined to explode. Each one of us, with our lives, will create an entire universe. Each one of us possesses a profoundly immense and unique potential. The question is this: will the universe we create be a true reflection of the potential we possess?

Rosh Hashanah is the day of judgment. Yet, never once during the prayers on Rosh Hashanah do we mention our past or ask for any kind of forgiveness. For this we wait until Yom Kippur. But that's odd — how can we be judged if we don't deal with our past deeds?

The answer is that we all make mistakes in life, mistakes that move us further and further from a realization of our potential as human beings and as Jews. If we are not wholeheartedly committed to pursuing a path to our ultimate potential, then we are inevitably doomed to repeat the mistakes of our past and find new ways to move ever further from our potential. From who we truly want to be. From who we truly *can* be.

Likewise, the dialectic of Rosh Hashanah and Yom Kippur. On Rosh Hashanah we refine the vision of our potential and commit to it. Then, and only then, can we ensure that the changes we make on Yom Kippur will be of a lasting nature.

There is a famous story about an elderly sage named Reb Zusia. Reb Zusia lay on his deathbed surrounded by his students and disciples. Reb Zusia was crying and there was no one who could comfort him.

One student implored, *"You were almost as wise as Moses himself"*, another followed, *"You were almost as kind as our father Abraham,"* and so on. Yet, Reb Zusia would not be comforted. He wept as the end drew near.

"When I pass from this world and appear before the heavenly tribunal," Reb Zusia said, *"they won't ask me, 'Zusia, why weren't you as wise as Moses or as kind as Abraham,' rather they will ask me 'why weren't you Zusia!' Why didn't I fulfill my potential, why didn't I follow the path that could have been mine."*

On Rosh Hashanah we confront our potential. As human beings, but even more, as Jews. The question is one of commitment. The issue is one of judgment.

9

THE SHOFAR SERVICE

Prelude to the Shofar
Psalm 47: To He Who Grants Victory

There are only two ways to build the tallest building. One, start building, or two, tear down all the others.

The challenge of life is not unlike that of fashioning a majestic structure. In Jewish thought, this challenge is a forty-nine step process.*

There are only two ways to reach our goals and realize our potential. One is by good old-fashioned dedication and persistence. The other is to redefine our potential as being that which we have already achieved. Simple, game over.

We read this Psalm seven times. In doing so we mention G-d's name forty-nine times. We are reminded to set our goals in life high, and to keep them there.

A Call for Clarity

The shofar is perhaps the most recognizable of all the Rosh Hashanah symbols. The sounding of the shofar plays a central role in the day's service. Young and old alike gather in a hush to listen carefully to the cry of the shofar.

1)   The commandment on Rosh Hashanah is to hear the sound

---

* The forty-nine days which elapsed between the exodus from Egypt and the receiving of the Torah at Mt. Sinai serve as a paradigm for this forty-nine step growth process. These are the forty-nine days which link the holidays of Passover and Shavuos and are known as the Sefira. Each day during this period is identified by a unique element of potential for personal growth and character development.

of the shofar. From the *Shema* we know that hearing in Judaism means to understand. The call of the shofar is the sound that wakes us up, so that we will make a choice for clarity, for awareness, for a fully constructive and purposeful life.

2) The blowing of the shofar consists of three sets of three different notes. Thus the minimum number of shofar blasts one is required to hear is nine — however, the accepted manner of blowing actually consists of many more. Each of the three notes *(Tekiah, Teruah, Shevarim)* is designed to evoke a particular idea and feeling.

> *Tekiah* (long note): This note calls us from the routines of day-to-day living, from a dissipation of our creative energies, to refocus ourselves on who it is we truly want to be.
>
> *Teruah* (short note): This note is more comforting. It softens us, allowing us to integrate the thoughts and feelings of the day.
>
> *Shevarim* (medium note): This is an anxious, longing note. Feel the tugging, the yearning to somehow start again, this time accomplishing what we want in life.

3) On the simplest, most basic level the sound of the shofar is the muffled cry of an injured soul. A soul crying for freedom. Free to be its own uninhibited self. The homing signal in every Jewish heart.

You That Slumber — Awake! A Shofar Essay

1)   Abraham, our forefather, stood on one side of the river and the entire world stood on the other. Abraham, the Midrash tells us, was able to take an unpopular stand against all of humanity. For truth, for meaning, for immutable values. For everything that is right and good. One man against the world. *"The deeds of the forefathers are a portent for the children."* We, the Jewish people,

are the spiritual heirs to the character, and the depth of being that Abraham possessed.

2)   The full force of the German people — the German war machine — was brought to bear on the objective of destroying the Jews. Yet somehow, in some inexplicable way, stories abound. Jews by the thousands and tens of thousands who refused to compromise their morality, their commitment to truth and meaning, and ultimately their commitment to G-d and Torah. A tortured and suffering people and all that they stood for, against a mighty and merciless enemy and all that it stood for.

The Jews were forced back against the barbed wire. The barbs pierced their flesh, pricking their bones, and the blood began to trickle and run. The Jews huddled and crowded together, stumbling and falling as more kept coming, colliding against the fallen ones and falling with them.

In the midst of this confusion the shrieking voice of the murderous chief was heard again:

"Sing, arrogant Jews, sing! Sing or you will die! Gunners, aim your machine guns! Now listen, you dirty Jews. Sing or you will die!"

And at that horrifying moment, one man pried himself loose from the frightened mob and broke the conspiracy of total silence. He stood there all alone and began to sing. His song was a chassidic folk song in which the chassid poured out his soul before the Almighty:

Lomir zich iberbeiten, iberbeiten,
Avinu shebashamayim,
Lomir zich iberbeiten, iberbeiten, iberbeiten — "
"Let us be reconciled, our Heavenly Father,
Let us be reconciled, let us make up — "

From Hassidic Tales of the Holocaust by Yaffa Eliach ©1982

A spark of song was kindled, but that spark fell short of its mark. The Jews had been beaten, and recoiled. The voice of the singer did not reach them. His song was silenced. There was no singing.

But something did happen at that moment. A change took place.

As soon as the solitary voice was hushed, humbly, another voice picked up the same tune, the same captivating chassidic tune. Only the words were not the same. New words were being sung. One solitary person in the entire humiliated and downtrodden crowd had become the spokesman of all the Jews. This man had composed the new song on the spot, a song derived from the eternal wellspring of the nation. The melody was the same ancient chassidic melody, but the words were conceived and distilled through the crucible of affliction:

> *"mir velen zey iberleben, iberleben,*
> *Avinu shebashamayim,*
> *Mir velen zey iberleben, iberleben, iberleben - "*
> *"We shall outlive them, our Heavenly Father,*
> *We shall outlive them, outlive them, outlive them - "*

This time the song swept the entire crowd. The new refrain struck like lightning and jolted the multitude. Feet rose rhythmically, as if by themselves. The song heaved and swelled like a tidal wave, arms were joined, and soon all the frightened and despondent Jews were dancing.

As for the commander, at first he clapped his hands in great satisfaction, laughing derisively. "Ha, ha, ha, the Jews are singing and dancing! Ha, ha, the Jews have been subdued!" But soon he grew puzzled and confused. What is going on? Is this how subdued people behave? Are they really oppressed and humiliated? They all seem to be fired up by this chassidic dance, as if they have forgotten all pain, suffering, humiliation, and despair. They have even forgotten about the presence of the Nazi commander . . .

"Stop, Jews! Stop at once! Stop the singing and dancing! Stop! Stop immediately!" the oppressor yelled out in a terrible voice, and for the first time his well-disciplined subordinates saw him at a loss, not knowing what to do next. "Stop! Stop! Stop at once!" the commander pleaded with his soldiers in a croaking voice. The Jews, singing and dancing ecstatically, were swept by the flood of their emotions and danced on and on. They paid a high price for it. They were brutally beaten for their strange behavior. But their singing and dancing did not stop.

3)   The world watched in awe. A tiny man was led across an obscure little bridge. A short walk from bondage to freedom. *"From the moment I decided never to make a moral compromise — I was a free man."* These were the words of Anatoly Sharansky. One small Jew who made a choice. The choice to stand for truth and for justice — even against the crushing power of his Soviet oppressors.

4)   The Jewish people have always taken a stand. For truth. For what is good and right. For pursuing that which we know to be meaningful — no matter where it may lead. Each one of us longs to take a stand. Deep within us all lies the strength and ability to take that stand. The shofar calls out to us. A call for clarity. To clarify for ourselves what we ultimately want. Who we want to be. What we really want to be committed to. The shofar sounds and stirs something deep within our heart and soul. We can sense the power. On Rosh Hashanah we can achieve it. The clarity and commitment. To stand alone as an individual and together as a people. To take a stand for everything the Jewish people represent. All we have to do is listen.

Wolf Fischelberg and his twelve-year-old son Leo were walking among the barracks of the sector for privileged people (Bevorzugenlager) in Bergen-Belsen, trying to barter some cigarettes for bread. As they were turning into another row of barracks, a stone was thrown across the barbed wire separating one sector from another. The stone flew over their heads and landed at their feet. It was clear that this was aimed at father and son.

"What does it mean?" Wolf turned to his son.

"Nothing! Just an angry Jew hurling stones," replied the son with a defiant note in his tone.

"Angry Jews do not cast stones; it is not part of our tradition," replied the father.

"Maybe it is time that it should become part of our tradition," the son snapped with restrained anger.

Wolf Fischelberg looked around to see if all was clear. Only then did he bend down to pick up the stone. A small gray note was wrapped around it. Wolf slipped the note into his pocket. They walked into a safe barracks where other Polish Jews lived. In a corner at a distance from the others, Wolf read the note. It was written in Hebrew by a Dutch Jew named Hayyim Borack, who had Argentinean papers. After establishing his credentials, Hayyim wrote that he was fortunate to have obtained a shofar and it was in his possession. If the chassidic Jews from the Polish transports wished to use the shofar for Rosh Hashanah services, Borack could smuggle the shofar in one of the coffee cauldrons of the morning distribution. In doing so they would lose a cauldron of coffee, for the shofar would be covered with a minimal amount of coffee, just enough to conceal it.

A vote was taken among the Polish Jews. Those in favor of the plan to smuggle in the shofar held a clear majority. They agreed to give up their morning coffee ration on the first day of Rosh Hashanah.

At the time and place specified in the note, a stone once more made its way over the electrified barbed-wire, this time from the Polish Jews to the Dutch. "You see, my son, Jews never throw stones in vain," said Wolf, as his eyes followed the stone making its way from one sector to another.

The smuggling of the shofar was a success. Nobody was caught and the shofar was not damaged. But now a new problem arose. In order to fulfill the mitzva, the obligation of shofar blowing, all present must clearly hear the voice of the shofar. The risk was great. If the sounds of the shofar reached German ears, all present would pay with their lives.

A heated debate developed among the scholars in the barracks as to whether one could properly fulfill the commandment of sounding the shofar if it could not be heard distinctly. In the absence of books, all discussants relied on their memory and quoted precedents from various Jewish sources. Based on Halakha (Jewish law), a decision was reached to blow the shofar quietly. G-d would surely accept the muffled sounds of the shofar and prayers of His sons and daughters just as He had accepted the prayers of Isaac atop the altar of Mount Moriah, thought Wolf Fischelberg as he was about to blow the shofar.

As little Miriam, Wolf's daughter, listened to the shofar, she hoped that it would bring down the barbed-wire fences of Bergen-Belsen, just as the blasts of the shofar had in earlier times made the walls of Jericho come tumbling down. The service was over. Nothing had changed. The barbed wires remained fixed in their places. Only in the heart did something stir — knowledge and hope: knowledge that the muffled voice of a shofar had made a dent in the Nazi wall of humiliation and slavery, and hope that someday freedom would bring down the barbed-wire fences of Bergen-Belsen and of humanity.

10

MUSSAF SERVICE: ESSENCE OF THE DAY

The Mussaf service, along with the sounding of the shofar, is the heart of the Rosh Hashanah prayers.

Mussaf is divided into three sections: Kingship (Malchiyos), Memories (Zichronos), and Shofar (Shofaros).

Kingship: Loyalty is the bedrock of any relationship. To be disloyal to a spouse, a friend, or to your country is to shatter the relationship. At this point in the service a Jew must consider where his loyalty ultimately lies.

Memories: Are there things you never forget to do? Push-ups in the morning, returning all your calls at work, telling your kids you love them? If you want to know what your priorities really are on a daily basis, then consider those things you always remember—even without setting the alarm on your watch.

Shofar: Wake up! It's time to rethink and recommit. Making sure that we remember where our loyalties lie and never forget the commitments we have made.

Repetition of the Mussaf

Unesaneh Tokef / Let Us Relate the Power of the Day

Most prayer books contain a brief account of the story behind this stirring passage which has become a highlight of the Rosh Hashanah service. It is the story of the great Rabbi Amnon who was slowly dismembered at the orders of a bishop rather than convert and deny his Judaism.

If being Jewish is worth dying for, then it is certainly worth living for.

Teshuva — Tefila — Tzedaka / Returning — Prayer — Charity

Do you ever feel that life is a juggling act? Trying your best to keep the balls in the air while your eyes dart this way and that to see what else may be flying towards you. All the while looking for a job — or a spouse. Raising kids — loving, laughing, and fighting. Easy, isn't it?

We all have three interwoven spheres of relationships in our lives. I and myself, I and G-d, and I and other human beings. Teshuva is a return to one's true path. To that sense of harmony — even hectic harmony — which flows from expressing your innermost self in the way you live. Prayer is returning to G-d. Charity is active concern for others.

Life is a three-legged pedestal. We struggle for balance.

Ata Zocher / You Remember

People say, "I want my children to have the things I never had." Should we not also say, "I want my child to be the person I never was."

How would you like to be remembered? As someone who was well dressed or well respected. As a taker or a giver.

We know how we want our children to be remembered, but do we know how they will remember us?

YOM KIPPUR

The Trees

11

PRAYER IS . . .

. . . A Multifaceted Discipline

It is at once childlike in its simplicity and profound beyond description. But that begs a question.

"How can I, having just taken leave of the roaring 80s and now embarking on the murky waters of the 1990s, relate to prayer in a meaningful way. In a way that I feel comfortable with. Because to be honest I do feel that there is something out there — call it G-d, call it the Force or whatever you want — and I do want to connect with whatever that something is. I just don't want to be left feeling like some weirded-out religious fanatic in the process."

This chapter contains six perspectives on prayer. Each one presents a different approach to relating to prayer. While these six are by no means exhaustive I do hope that at least one of them will open a path for you to have a genuine encounter with one of the richest treasures of Jewish life.

In the final analysis we need to understand that prayer is a highly sophisticated discipline which is not easily mastered. In its fullest sense it demands a lifetime of careful attention and effort. However, there is no doubt that even one sincere moment of prayer is laden with potential for the most moving of experiences.

It is my deepest wish that this chapter will provide a thoughtful and sensitive stepping stone into the world of prayer on Rosh Hashanah, on Yom Kippur, and throughout your lifetime.

. . . Self-inquiry

In Hebrew the most common term for praying is *lehitpalel*. This word, *lehitpalel*, is a reflexive verb that literally means to examine and judge oneself. The particular objects of our scrutiny are our attitudes and actions.

It is axiomatic to any process of inquiry and assessment that there must exist some basic standard or criteria against which judgment will be made. For instance, if you take your watch to a jeweler and ask the simple question, "Is this a good watch?" the jeweler can only give a meaningful reply if he has a standard of quality and craftsmanship against which to judge. At one end of his scale is a ten dollar throw-away watch and at the other extreme is a top-of-the-line Rolex. The issue is where on this continuum your watch fits in.

This perspective on prayer uses the words and concepts embodied in the prayer book as "top-of-the-line" standards against which we hold up our feelings, attitudes, and actions. We reflect on where we fit in, consider why we measure up the way we do, take this to heart and think about how we can improve.

In life it is essential to know "where you stand." Be it on the job, in a relationship, or on a particular social or political issue. In Jewish life you must also know where you stand. If we read in the daily prayer book the words — *sound the great shofar for our freedom, raise a banner to gather our exiles and speedily gather us together from the four corners of the earth to our land* — then we have to ask ourselves: (a) Besides my checks to various worthy causes am I really bothered by the fact that there are Jews in Syria or Yemen who are unable to emigrate to Israel? (b) How bothered? Have I ever cried at the thought of a Jewish mother whose husband languishes in prison for no reason? (c) *Vekabtzenu*/and gather us . . . *L'artzenu*/to our land. Do I really think of Israel as my home? Would I be proud of my children if they chose to settle there? Do I in any way long for the Jewish people to be united again in Jerusalem?

These are not easy or comfortable questions, but then again self-assessment never is. In order to grow you must first know where you stand. When using this approach to prayer I suggest you choose one or two concepts to focus on each time you pray. You can either decide ahead of time which concepts they will be or you can play it by ear as the prayer service progresses. In either case the idea is quality and not quantity. One concept is certainly sufficient if you earnestly reflect on it. This approach can open up a whole world of self-discovery as well as personal, spiritual, and Jewish growth.

. . . An Instrument for Change

There is a question which students of Jewish thought have been asking for centuries. The question is this. "If (as Judaism claims) whatever G-d does for us is exactly what is best for us then why do we ever ask for anything in our prayers? Isn't what we already have precisely what we need?"

The approach to dealing with this question is quite telling in terms of the Jewish view of what human beings should be doing with their lives. (This question also raises other sensitive issues, but for now we will deal only with how it relates to prayer.) Judaism sees life as a steady stream of opportunities for learning, growing, and changing. This is known as *tikkun ha-middot*, or the constant refinement of human character and deed that comes through ever-increasing self-awareness. In the vernacular we call it *"working on yourself."*

The answer to our original question stems from this slice of Jewish weltanschauung and is as follows. If I grow and change throughout the course of my life, if in terms of my attitudes, inclinations and actions I transcend my former self, then what is best for me will also change. In other words, prayer itself is an experiential medium for effecting personal growth. Therefore, the fact that I can make requests during prayer tells me that I ought to be a different person after prayer than when I began. What was best for me when I began is not necessarily what is best for me when I have finished.

If this is so then there is a follow-up question which must also be asked. How is it that prayer can affect personal growth and change?

Consider if you will the annual phenomenon of New Year's resolutions. I would like to suggest that the reason these resolutions rarely last is not because they were unrealistic or because unforeseen obstacles arose, but because the initial commitment was only half-hearted. And a half-hearted commitment is no commitment at all.

Our sages taught us that *"all beginnings are difficult."* The first step to achieving anything meaningful in life is the commitment to do so. If your commitment is resolute then you have already overcome your greatest obstacle to success. The rest is all but guaranteed.

As we read and take to heart the values and ideals expressed in the language of the prayers we must always ask ourselves — "do I really mean what I am saying?" That means — am I truly committed to the values I am now uttering, or is this just lip service.

The opportunity is growth, the essential ingredient is commitment, and the means is prayer.*

... Talking to G-d

Four out of five people in America say that G-d answers their prayers. What about you? Have you ever prayed and really meant it? Have you ever spoken to G-d or cried out to Him from the depths of your being? Did He answer you?

---

* Keep in mind that in prayer we are having a personal encounter with G-d. He knows if we mean it or not, so don't kid yourself — if you don't mean it then don't commit. But if you do — then do it all the way.

E=MC² is a relatively simple equation. It is also one of the most penetrating notions to ever occupy the human mind. Prayer is also quite simple. G-d is here and you can speak to Him. That's all there is to it. No tricks, no intermediaries, just talk. Is there anything more simple — is there anything more magnificent?

G-d is the designer and creator of the universe. The source of all existence. The stars that blanket the sky, the stately snowcapped peaks and the waves crashing on the rocky coast. All of this and more. And it all pales to nothingness in the face of its creator. This creator. This G-d. You can speak to Him. At this very moment you are in His presence. You can learn to feel that. You can touch the ultimate.

But there is a part of us that is afraid. "What if I speak to Him and *I do* feel a presence. Then what will happen to me?" Or perhaps you just feel sort of, well, weird. Awkwardly out of place. That all makes sense. Look, you're not used to this. Don't worry though — G-d won't bite you. Like anything else it will take practice and patience but in the end there is obviously nothing more sublime than speaking to G-d.

Once there was a king whose son wanted to go out into the world. He wanted to travel, to explore and make it on his own. After some time he found that he was desperately short of cash and that his credit cards had all expired. He was far, far away from his father's kingdom, in a land whose ways and language were very different from his own. In a moment many years passed and he became a successful and respected citizen in his new homeland. Then, one day, a feeling overcame him. He wanted to go home. To see his father again. And so he took leave for another long journey. After many months he was again on the soil of his father's kingdom. It was a land whose ways and tongue he had forgotten. There he stood at the entrance to the palace. Alone. Unable to

> *communicate or to identify himself. He was home but he was still so very lost. From beneath a window to his father's chamber he desperately cried out in his foreign tongue — faa-ther, faa-ther! So many lost years flashed through his mind. His voice cracked in helplessness. Inside the chamber the king heard a frightful cry. He did not know the language, but that voice — even after so long — he knew the voice of his son. They wept as they embraced. Welcome home son, welcome home.*

G-d is waiting to hear our voices. The words and the language really don't matter. Only to hear the voice of a child. We can talk to Him. Even if it's just a few whispered words. "G-d, I'm home." Don't worry, it's okay. Tell G-d that you feel a little uncomfortable but that you really do want to feel close. Tell Him that you know He's there, you know He's listening and that you want to come home.

It may take awhile but eventually you will see. There is nothing as simple, or as exalted, as being home.

. . . Your Inner Life

The worst thing about the proverbial glass house is not its susceptibility to stones but rather its dramatic lack of privacy. I know a woman who is a psychologist working with prisoners in a state-run maximum-security facility. She tells me that in prison there is a horrific lack of privacy. Even in the bathroom there are no walls around you or doors to close. Just a dank room full of cold ceramic toilets where other men sit and stare at you. This, she says, breeds a terrible rage that tears away at every prisoner's soul.

We all lead two lives and live in two worlds. An outer life and an inner life. One public and one private.

After the bank teller says, *"Good morning"* and asks how she can help, how do you respond? With a prerecorded *"I'm fine thanks, how are you . . ."* only then to drone on about the transactions you would like to execute, or, even in the midst of a world drowning in computer printouts where people deal with one another like so many PINs, do you respond to this person, well, like a person?

There must be a part of your life which is secluded and private. Not an external hiding place, but a chamber within your heart. An internal study to which to retreat. To contemplate, to talk to G-d or just to hear yourself breathe.

Rabbi Shlomo Volbe, possessor of the type of ennobled heart and mind which is unique to the holy city of Jerusalem, describes prayer as *"sudden quietness."* Prayer is a rite of visitation to that private place in your heart and it is from there that your equilibrium will flow. In prayer we take the ideas expressed in the words and thoughtfully meditate on them. We try to understand them and to feel them. To let them permeate our being and become a part of who we are. Prayer is the guarantor of our inner lives. It is that which preserves and nourishes the indispensable private domain of heart and soul. Without that privacy we can slide into a silent rage — or more likely — shrivel up and die.

. . . Being Connected to the Jewish People

Did you ever notice that the bulk of our prayers, in fact the entire Amidah, are in the plural? Help *us*, save *us*, return *us*, and so on.

I remember being in Paris with a backpack on my back and a kippa on my head. I was not quite twenty-one and I was engaged in that hallowed rite of passage known as looking for oneself. As if some spiritual clone of every young American lives in a quaint loft somewhere in Europe.

The most phenomenal thing happened to me in Paris. Wherever I went I was besieged by a curious mix of Parisian Jews. None of them looked particularly Jewish, they just sort of stepped out from the sea of faces that filled the avenues of Paris.

"Would you like to come to my house for dinner?" one of them asked.

"Do you need a place to sleep?" inquired another.

"Can I help you? . . . Do you need directions? . . . Take my number in case you need anything . . ." I was even offered money!

All of this from Jews to whom I was a complete stranger. But there I was, like so many others, roaming the streets of Paris and thinking about life. There was only one difference, the kippa on my head. And thus, we were one. One people and one family. Inexorably bound together.

And so when we pray we do so in the plural. Because each one of us is a part of a greater organism. A living cell in a body that is 3,000 years young. We pray in the plural because we exist in them as they exist in us.

. . . Tuning into the Cosmos

A carpenter uses a hammer and nails, a writer his ink and quill, but what does G-d use when He wants to fashion a universe? There is a fantastically expressive Jewish idea which says that the tools that G-d used for creation were the very letters of the Hebrew alphabet. In fact the first thing G-d created was the letters and then He used them to construct the rest of existence.

The Hebrew language is a multilayered superstructure containing limitless nuances, each reflecting a different dimension of insight. Each Hebrew letter has numerous levels of meaning. Let us use the letter *aleph,* the first letter in the alphabet, as an archetype.

1)   The *aleph,* because it is the first letter in the alphabet, has a numerical value of one. It follows that *beit,* the second letter, would have a numerical value of two and so on throughout the alphabet. G-d, as the Jewish people taught the world, is one.

2)   Each letter is also a word and thus incorporates the concept which that word expresses. The word *aleph* expresses the

concept of leadership or to champion. A military commander is an *aluf*.

3) The Talmud teaches that each letter contains an idea related to the first time the letter appears in the Torah as the first letter of a word. The first time *aleph* appears as the first letter of a word is *elohim*, which is one of G-d's names. Therefore the *aleph* signifies an aspect of G-dliness.

4) The form of the letter itself. An *aleph*, when written in a Torah scroll, is actually a composite of two *yuds* and a *vav*. The letter *yud* represents the unity of G-d and has the numerical value of 10. The *vav* in Hebrew serves as a grammatical link: *vav* as a prefix means "and," thus connecting two thoughts. *Vav* has the numerical value of 6.

- The *aleph* is written with one *yud* above the *vav* and the other below it. "*Aleph*" (the leader) and "*aleph*" (the embodiment of divinity) and "*aleph*" (which is the numeral 1, like G-d who is both the first cause as well as being "one") is embodied in a form which portrays G-d's unity in sovereignty. The G-d of the heavenly, spiritual sphere is the same as the G-d below in the earthly realm.

- Also, the numerical value of two *yuds* (10 + 10) plus *vav* (6) is 26, which is equivalent to the ineffable name of G-d that represents His transcendent unity.

The Hebrew letters and words are far more than symbolic images and sounds. Each letter is a living organism. These primordial letters of creation gave birth to the totality of existence. Contained within each letter are not only hidden meanings but hidden capabilities as well.

The early sages who composed our prayers held within their minds and souls the keys with which to unlock the creative forces concealed in the Hebrew language.

When we speak, we create. We create impressions, feelings, ideas and even revolutions. Simply through the force of our words. On a much deeper level the authors of our prayers knew how to use the letters and words in such a way that they would work to attune our souls and connect us to G-dliness. Beyond the manifest meaning of the words lies a coded message, a spiritual software package that works to direct and connect our souls in ways we are unaware.

Prayer, particularly in Hebrew, has the capacity to help us touch and be affected by a spiritual reality that is far beyond the purview of our ordinary means of comprehension.*

---

* Judaism is clear in its assertion that a person can pray in any language. However, there are dimensions of the prayer experience which can never survive a translation from Hebrew. A recommended starting point for one who hopes to eventually pray in Hebrew is to begin by learning and even memorizing the first paragraph of the *Shema* as well as the first paragraph of the *Amidah*.

12

KOL NIDRE: THE CREDIBILITY FACTOR

Tefila Zakka

*O*ne winter morning my wife noticed that a small envelope had been dropped by our back door. No name, no address, nothing. Inside was a thank-you note. A few words had been written in haste with a signature that was barely legible.

Our backyard serves as an occasional shortcut or meeting place for some of our neighbors. We're new on the block and it seems we are centrally located in the midst of some old neighborhood friends.

My wife tacked the card to the bulletin board in our hallway. In a day or two she would ask a neighbor if it was theirs. Weeks and months passed as did the long winter nights. As for the card, it got lost on that bulletin board, covered by a sea of coupons and school notices.

Autumn is beautiful where we live: the streets, particularly ours, are adazzle with colors. Fiery reds, oranges and yellows of every shade. One day there was a knock on the door. It was that man everyone sees but no one knows. You see him all over town riding that wobbly, rusted bicycle laden with old bags and rags full of G-d knows what — probably more bags and rags. The elements don't seen to faze him, he just keeps on peddling.

"Would you like me to rake your leaves?" he asked. Sure I said, why not. At least he has enough self-respect to try and earn some money. Besides, he had once shoveled the snow from our driveway and did a pretty good job. My wife cautioned, though — let's keep the girls inside while he's working out there — these days, sadly, you just never know.

Autumn passed, as did Succos and Chanukah. Before you knew it the snows had returned. Winter too has a beauty all its own and we were blessed with one of those storms that blankets a city with early morning silence.

The girls and I were outside building snowmen, one for each child. A big one for our 5 year old, a smaller one for our 2 ½ year old and a tiny one for the baby. "Excuse me sir," came the voice of the man on the bicycle, "would you like me to shovel your drive?" Why not, I thought — help the guy out, not to mention myself. He was shoveling and we were having the time of our lives. My 2 ½ year old, as friendly and curious as can be, asked him, "What's your name?" "J.D.," he replied, "what's yours?"

Later, as we were putting the final touches on our snow-kids, my daughter said, "Abba, I love J.D., he's a nice man." "He sure is," I said, and we went inside to warm up and have some lunch.

Back in the house my wife had made a couple of sandwiches to give to the man on the bicycle when he finished his work. "Mommy," the little one said, "I love J.D." "That's nice," she said, but neither of us wanted her to feel too good about this nice, but curious stranger.

> *A week or so later, after J.D. had shoveled for the second time that winter, my wife found herself doing one of those tasks she had been postponing for months. She was clearing off the bulletin board in the hall. Away with old school notices and expired coupons — up with a new schedule of community lectures. She put aside that faceless thank-you card. It will be embarrassing, she thought, but I'll ask the neighbors if it's theirs anyway.*
>
> *The card fell open on the table and she read it. "Thank you for your help and your kindness," signed, "J.D."*

We still haven't gotten over that thank-you card. That first winter when the man on the bicycle had shoveled our drive we didn't even know his name. I had paid him nicely and my wife gave him a container of chicken that was left over from Shabbos. He reluctantly took the chicken — he still had his pride — thanked us for the work and wobbled off on his overloaded bicycle through the snowy streets.

Who is he? Where does he live? Does he have a family? One thing I do know — he went to a lot of effort just to buy a thank-you note and return to our house to drop it at our back door.

Says a lot about "J.D." — doesn't it?

* * *

It's hard to be forgiving. Throughout the course of the year, in one way or another, people hurt us. Emotionally, physically, monetarily. In the vast majority of instances the hurt passes, leaving few if any enduring marks. Or, we may realize, it was actually our honor — our ego — that was more bruised than anything else. Yet it is still hard to forgive.

What about us? Did you hurt anyone this year? Knowingly or perhaps without even realizing it at the time. We're human, we live, how can it be that we don't step on a few toes or overlook a few sentiments, a few feelings that others hold dear. It's so hard to forgive, but it's nothing like asking for forgiveness. We so want to be perfect, and to say "I'm sorry" is to dredge up a thousand shortcomings. It can be so humbling, so very unappealing.

The *Tefila Zakka* is an often overlooked little prayer said just before *Kol Nidre* on Yom Kippur Eve. There we are in synagogue, we're late, we're exchanging New Year's greetings or checking out the latest style in ties or dresses — we just don't have time for Tefila Zakka — after all, doesn't Yom Kippur really begin with Kol Nidre anyway.

Tefila Zakka contains one of the most important prayers we will say throughout the entire Yom Kippur service. Quite simply it is a paragraph which says, ". . . since I know that there is no righteous person in the world who does not sin against his fellow man, either monetarily or physically, in deed or in speech, therefore my heart aches within me . . . May no person be punished on my account. And just like I forgive everyone so may you grant me favor in every person's eyes that they may also grant me full forgiveness."

Sure, we hurt people during the year, but that's not us. We don't want to be a source of pain or hardship in someone else's life. In a few instances we may have said we're sorry, but most times we just gloss them over. We hope and pray that people will forgive us. That they will look beyond the surface. That they will know that in truth there is so much more to who I am than that moment of pain I inflicted. And we too must try to look beyond the surface. To know that each person is really a world. Complex and confounding. To themselves as well as others.

Tefila Zakka can bring us so close. To others, and to ourselves as well. Isn't that how Yom Kippur should really begin?

Kol Nidre

If there is anything which you vowed to do this year and now realize that you cannot live up to your word — this is *Kol Nidre*.

There are probably more Jews in synagogue for *Kol Nidre* than at any other time during the year. The question is, why? What is it about *Kol Nidre* that keeps the crowds coming back?

Could it possibly be that consciously or unconsciously every Jew senses that *Kol Nidre* touches the most sensitive nerve of their humanity. That without *Kol Nidre* you can't have a Yom Kippur. That without *Kol Nidre* you can't have a life.

In *Kol Nidre* we make this statement: I realize that if I have made any verbal commitments, if I gave my word on anything, then without recourse to some higher authority there is no backing out. My word is my word — period. My word locks into place a reality which I can no longer undo. That reality — that word — binds me.

Imagine a world where contracts didn't have to be signed. Where a person's word was "as good as gold" and a handshake was a done deal. Imagine if people actually lived with that kind of trust in one another. Imagine the integrity.

Beyond the elimination of mountains of paperwork and half the legal profession, it would be a different world. There is no other way to describe it. An entirely different world.

Kol Nidre is a time when we take a searing look inside. We ask ourselves — who can count on my word. Can my children, or my spouse? My friends, my boss? Can G d? Can I! Can I count on my own word — do I trust myself?

Without credibility we have nothing. With it — we have everything. Thus, *Kol Nidre*.

13

TESHUVA: FOUR STEPS TO GREATNESS

My brother was 15 when he bought his first horse. Unlike other kids who rode bicycles, skateboards, or motorcycles, my brother preferred a horse. Now this was no ordinary horse. This was an imposing jet black thoroughbred named Seriously, a retired race horse.

I took him up on his offer and decided to take Seriously for a ride around the neighborhood. A ride that was almost my last. Not far from my parents' home was a long, wide boulevard which featured expansive grassy islands running down the middle of the road. On one side of these islands traffic flowed in one direction and on the other side it moved in the opposite direction. In between each island was a crossover point so that cars could cut through and change direction. It was one of those crossover points that was almost my doom.

As you can well imagine, when old Seriously reached the top of that long open stretch of grass he had a sudden flash of deja vu. There he was again, a young virile thoroughbred poised at the starting gate ready to impress the world with his speed and power. And *there sat I, the unsuspecting victim of this wishful leap back to the days of one horse's youth.*

A bloodcurdling scream was lodged in my throat and Seriously was off to the races. The harder I pulled on those reins and the more violently I kicked at his ribs, the less he paid attention to me. Faster and faster he galloped. We were closing in on one of those crossover points and it was clear that the horse had absolutely no intention of stopping to look both ways before crossing. Through the horrified tears in my eyes I could see that a red Cadillac and a new Mercedes sports car were both using the crossover and were totally oblivious to the horse and rider headed their way. At least, I thought, I'd go out in style.

To make a long story short, I survived, though I don't think I've mounted a horse since.

Today, my brother lives on a farm with his wife and baby, raises some chickens, owns a goat named Blacky, and still rides his horse whenever he gets a chance. What's amazing to me is that he can do it bareback. Without any need for a saddle or even reins. He just jumps up and is instantly one with the animal. It responds to his commands and takes him — with more grace and power than he could ever muster — wherever he wants to go. He is the picture of a rider in perfect control of his horse. And me, well, I already told you that story.

Body and Soul: Want vs. Feel

When our sages wanted to find an image that would capture the internal dynamics of human life they chose our very own horse and rider. This is their picture of man and of the human condition.

There is a basic tension in life which we all feel. That tension is between what we *want* to do and what we *feel* like doing. Does this ring a bell, do you recognize the tension? *I want* to help my son with his homework — I *feel* like relaxing in front of the TV. I *want* to lose 15 pounds — I *feel* like having a piece of cheesecake. I *want* to visit my parents — I *feel* like playing tennis. I *want* to make a difference with my life — I *feel* like just getting by and minding my own business. I *want* greatness — I *feel* like settling for being average.

The rider, what we want to do, that's our soul. The horse, what we feel like doing, that's our body. Mind you, Judaism never denigrates the body or physical pleasures. Quite the opposite. Judaism says that the pleasures of the physical world are here to be enjoyed. To be fully partaken of. There is just one catch: who is in control. Is this a skilled rider leading a faithful obedient horse, or is this a rider who has lost control and is at the mercy of his horse's every whim and desire?

The Mistakes We Make

We all make mistakes. Almost everyday we do things that we really don't want to be doing. It's a fascinating phenomenon.

When was the last time you had the following experience? You were confronted with the opportunity to do something which you perceived as being wrong, something you clearly did not want to do. But a funny thing happened on the way to Yom Kippur. That very act which you didn't want to commit — you did it anyway. Fascinating. Before you did it you knew it was a mistake and you didn't want to do it. While you were doing it you knew it was a mistake and you didn't want to be doing it and after the fact you looked back in wonderment. Not feeling very good about yourself. You pondered, "Why did I do that?"

The answer is this. We are all geniuses. Everyone of us. When it comes to our ability to rationalize, the Einstein in all of us begins to surface. We are capable of the most convincing bits of intellectual dexterity, temporarily tying our minds in one convoluted knot after another, thereby enabling ourselves to do what we feel like doing instead of what we really want to do.

This is the root of many of the mistakes we make in life. We all *want* to do what's right. Only sometimes we rationalize and do what we *feel* like instead.

Defining Our Terms

One of the most common words in your prayer book is *sin.* Not a very pleasant sounding word. Certainly no one wants to look at themselves as a sinner. In Hebrew, the generic term for sin is *chet.* This term literally means, "to make a mistake." Sins, no thanks. But mistakes — sure — we all make mistakes.

The issue on Yom Kippur is this: how do we correct the mistakes of our past and avoid repeating them in the future? If we can understand this, then we possess the key to unlocking an enormous reservoir of latent potential for greatness which would otherwise lie dormant.

This is *teshuva.* The common translation of teshuva is repentance. Again, a rather foreign sounding idea. The proper translation of the word teshuva is — *to return.* Teshuva is an animated technique for locating the rationalizations that lie at the root of our mistakes — recognizing them, dealing with them and eliminating them.

Four Steps to Teshuva — Four Steps to Greatness

1) Regret *(charata)* —

Regret — as opposed to guilt.

Regret is that state of vexation in which one feels a sense of loss. If you misplace your wallet with a thousand dollars in it, you feel regret, not guilt. You have lost something of value.

In our striving for growth we must first see that our mistakes in life have resulted in the loss of something we deem to be dear and important.

2) Abandonment *(aziva)* —

As General Schwarzkopf once put it: *"Gentleman, all I can say is we identified the target in question and it no longer exists."*

I lost my wallet, or worse yet, I lost a friend, now how do I avoid repeating the same mistake? Once you feel the loss it's then time to set out on a mission of search and destroy. You must identify the rationalization, see what it was that enticed you into that cerebral snare, and understand the basic untruth that is the nucleus of rationalization.

Now, you must issue a cease and desist order. Stop the rationalization and put a halt to the action it sanctioned.

3) Confession *(vidduy)* —

In other words — *"now go and say you're sorry."* There is perhaps no greater torture in a child's mind than being told he has to apologize. Stick bamboo shoots under my nails, tie me to the rack — anything — but don't make me say I'm sorry!

Because when you verbalize your regret it makes everything all too real, like being on a darkened stage with the spotlight on you. There is no escape. The truth about your actions and their hurtful consequences are laid bare for all to see when you utter those simple words — *"I'm sorry . . . I feel awful about what I did, it won't happen again — I promise."*

4) Resolve *(kabala)* —

Say what you mean — *"I'm sorry."* And mean what you say — *"It won't happen again."* With this final act of commitment never to repeat the same mistake, you have come full circle. You have returned.

If a friend comes and you see that he sincerely regrets what he did, that he understands his mistake, wishes it had never happened and with a heavy heart apologizes and pledges never to repeat it, would you not be immediately forgiving?

What if that friend was your son — or — what if that son was you?

Practical Application

One of the pitfalls inherent in Yom Kippur is biting off more than you can chew. I would therefore like to offer some practical suggestions.

1) Look at your life in terms of three spheres of relationships. One with yourself, one with G-d, and one with other people.

2) Make a list of five mistakes you have made in each sphere and rank them from most to least serious.

3) Take that list with you to synagogue on Yom Kippur and plan a strategy for the day. For example: On Yom Kippur night you will take one of your top three mistakes through the four-step process.* During the morning service, you will concentrate on the next two — and so on. You must learn to pace yourself. This isn't easy and comes only with years of practice.

4) Create mental strategies for the coming year. It can be overwhelming to attempt too many immediate changes or to try and correct all your mistakes at once. Therefore, even for those which you won't address on Yom Kippur you should nonetheless try to construct a plan of action for when you will deal with them during the year.

5) Keep your list of mistakes in a private place but make sure you won't lose track of it. You should review this list for 15 minutes once a month.

6) Remember that teshuva is a unique mitzva. With other mitzvot (commandments) if you are lacking part of the mitzva you lack the whole thing. An esrog and a lulav are made up of four species, but if you are missing one, it is as if you have nothing. With regards to teshuva, every effort you make and every step you take brings you closer to

---

*Regarding mistakes where you have hurt or wronged another person, it is most appropriate to ask that person for forgiveness before Yom Kippur.

where you want to be. No one can ever take away a step of
progress, a step of growth or a step towards greatness.

14

HIGHLIGHTS OF THE YOM KIPPUR MORNING SERVICE

Birchas Hashachar / Morning Blessings

Asher Yatzar / Who Has Designed Man with Wisdom

I have a friend and anyone who knows him will tell you — he's driven. The man simply operates at a different level of intensity than you or I. So I asked, "What happened, what is it that lights your fire . . ."

This is the story he told me:

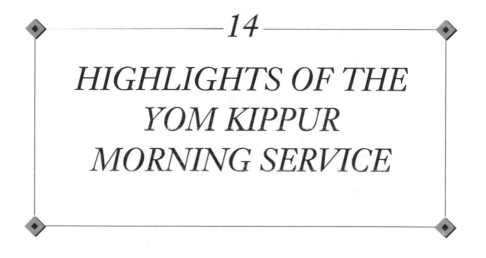

I was in high school and my parents were going away for the weekend. "Michael," my father asked, "do me a favor and finish painting the garage this weekend." I agreed.

Not long after my parents pulled out of the driveway did another car with three of my friends pull in. "But Mike, you know how beautiful the woods are this time of year . . ." It wasn't an easy decision, but I opted out.

Later that evening I was informed that my friends had all died in a horrible collision. I was a survivor, still am, driven for the rest of my life. Because I know, I know I've got a mission.

We are all survivors. And, as long as we possess the gift we call life, we have a mission.

Think about who you are. Your unique circumstance in life. Strengths, weaknesses and special abilities. For yourself and for your family. For the Jewish people and for all mankind. We all have a mission.

Birchas HaTorah / Blessings for the Torah

There are 613 commandments in the Torah. Among them are love your neighbor as yourself, do not murder, and love G-d.

The Talmud states that if you could put 612 commandments on one end of a scale and just one commandment on the other end, there is one commandment which would outweigh all the rest.

This is the commandment to study the wisdom of the Torah. How many things can you think of that are more essential than acquiring wisdom. The insights necessary to build a close and loving marriage, to raise children, to maintain friendships and to get the most out of life.

Wisdom. Understanding. Insight. The ultimate commandment.

Pesukei D'Zimrah

Hallu Es Hashem / Praise G-d from the Heavens

Our sages say, "there is no artist like our G-d"
We know that, just look around.

Which is more beautiful, the tree in front of your home or the painting of a tree in a gallery? As wondrous as a painting may be it is a mere approximation of reality. Yet we think nothing of a group of people staring at a painting, but put that same group of people in front of a tree on my lawn and I immediately dial 911 for help.

The painting is a reminder. No, it's a window. It keys us into the infinite beauty of a tree. The tree too is a window. Step through, for the infinite lies beyond.

Yishtabach / May Your Name Be Praised

This is the closing prayer in the *Pesukei D'Zimrah*, the preparatory portion of the morning prayer service.

There are fifteen expressions of praises to G-d in this paragraph. In the Temple in Jerusalem there were fifteen ascending steps. We must deal with our relationship with G-d — the infinite — as we deal with life, one step at a time. Sure, you can bound up a stairway two steps at a time, but don't try it in life. Each step is a message, a lesson. An indispensable part of the chorus of experiences which shape and mold who you are — your character — and who you will become.

So too our spiritual lives. Our relationship with G-d. Multifaceted, subtle and sublime. Our inner lives too must be fashioned one step at a time.

Fifteen expressions of "praise" for G-d. Ever higher, ever deeper. New and more stirring moments of intimacy. Each one predicated on the last, each one embracing the other.

Life is so busy, it moves so quickly. Our minds entertain a volume of thoughts in the blink of an eye. Our hearts, feelings enough to fill the oceans, and then there is our soul. Longing, yearning evermore. Every moment. To live.

* * *

You are about to enter the main body of the morning prayer service. It will open up with *Borachu,* wind its way to *Shema* and culminate with the *Amidah,* the standing prayer. As you turn from page to page and from prayer to prayer, make sure you're not alone. Take your innerself with you. Your heart, your soul, whatever it is that you feel as the ineffable you.

Take a moment or two. Don't be afraid. Close your eyes and calm your breath. Now feel with that other sense, that inner you, and listen with that other ear to the silent sounds. There is so much inside of us at any given moment. So far beyond comprehension, or so it seems. Now is the time to know, to whatever degree you can, who you are and to feel the pulse of your life — and now — to move onward.

Borachu / **Bless G-d**

Even an atheist will tell you, ". . . if there is a G-d, that would be *it*. To relate to Him, to be close to Him, that would be the ultimate pleasure, what life is really all about."

G-d is infinite. And like infinity G-d defies our comprehension. G-d, like infinity, can never be added to. He can never become more, He can receive nothing.

With borachu we don't "bless" G-d, we don't give Him anything, rather we recognize that He is the source of all existence and of all blessing. He only gives and we can only receive.

This is truly humbling. Like the master and the disciple. The greater the humility — which is no less than a recognition of the reality — the greater the capacity to imbibe the craft in all its subtlety, the wisdom in all its shades. Such is the ultimate paradox. The less we know we are, the greater we can become.

Shema Yisroel / **Hear O Israel**

When a Jew dies, he dies with the *Shema* on his lips. But why — what is the meaning of this indelible bit of Jewish consciousness?

Moments before execution a prisoner is offered a final meal, a last cigarette. When we say the *Shema* we cover our eyes and see ourselves dying — with the *Shema* on our lips.

Don't you see? It's one last chance to grab hold of what life was all about to begin with.

Make a list in your mind. Your three greatest pleasures in life. Then ask yourself — what is the pleasure? What is the essence of that moment, the experience that allows me to feel such pleasure?

If you seek then you will surely find. It's all the same thing. *"Echad,"* oneness. A pristine unity. A beautiful harmony. List your pleasures —

> Friendship — *"echad,"* oneness.
>
> Acquiring knowledge — *"echad,"* to unify.
>
> Nature — *"echad,"* to feel at one with.

Love — *"echad,"* to become one.

Skiing — *"echad,"* one with the mountain.

And so on. . . . *"echad."*

V'Haya Iym Shemoah / **And If You Listen**

In the second paragraph of the *Shema* we find the words, ". . . *and you will eat and be satisfied — be careful . . . "*

Food, clothing and shelter. Once your basic needs are taken care of, then what? It seems our society has answered that question by saying — "more of the same."

Food, how about nouvelle cuisine, Mexican or thirty-two flavors of ice cream. Clothing, just take a stroll down any Mall Street U.S.A. Shelter, an endless array of shapes and sizes with decor and appliances to match. When our society answered the question of "now what" with "more of the same," that was a choice with far-reaching consequences. For individuals, families, society and even the planet we inhabit.

"*. . . and you will eat and be satisfied — be careful . . . "* Now that your basic needs have been met, what are your priorities. And what does that tell you about who you are.

At this point in the Shema we focus on the role of *mitzvot*, commandments. Kabbalistic literature defines the word commandments *(mitzvot)* as "bits of advice." Each commandment advises us as to what our priorities ought to be, how to stay focused and how to realize the goals embodied in those priorities.

Amidah / The Standing Prayer

Hashem Sefasai Tiftach / **G-d Open My Lips**

A little girl's first tentative steps, she thinks she can not walk, but she can. A child fears he will never swim, but he will. Many of our limitations in life are more perceived than real. It is only ghosts which are holding us back.

In Hebrew the word for lips is the same as for *banks,* as in *river banks*. The banks of a river define its limitations. When we say, "G-d, open my lips," we are also saying, "G-d, help me to see beyond my perceived limitations."

Baruch Ata Hashem / Blessed Are You O G-d

The essence of all Jewish prayer and of all Jewish life is contained in the first few words of the *Amidah.* The word to focus on is *ata,* "you." We address G-d directly. Prayer is no less than personal time with G-d. To speak to Him. Honestly, openly and from the heart. This is the key to everything.

Elokai, Ad Shelo Notzarti / My G-d, Before I Was Formed

Ants build anthills, beavers build dams and we build the World Trade Center. In the ultimate scheme of things is there really a difference?

In the end the stoic forces of nature will wash away all traces of the anthill and the civilization it housed. Piece by piece the dam will slowly rot or the river itself will become dry and lifeless. What of our monuments? Are they not mere relics for the future?

We are to the universe and to time what the ant is to our planet. All but nothing. A speck of dust lost in history. With one difference — ants don't speak to G-d. What they say or do doesn't really matter. But our thoughts, our words, and our actions do make a difference. An eternal difference.

15

THE FOREST AND THE TREES

A Vidduy Essay

The year was 1882 and Oscar Wilde was coming to the United States. The customs official routinely inquired if he had anything to declare. His reply: "Only my genius." Years later as he sat in prison and reflected on a squandered life, Mr. Wilde mused, "I have been a spendthrift of my genius . . . I forgot that every little action of the common day makes or unmakes character."

One of the most striking differences between Rosh Hashanah and Yom Kippur revolves around attention to detail. On Rosh Hashanah we grapple with life's ultimate issues — Who am I? Where do I want my life to go and what is the legacy I hope to leave? Yom Kippur on the other hand is a day in which attention to detail reigns supreme. Throughout the sections of the service which deal with *vidduy* — confession — (i.e. *Ashamnu* and *Al-chet*) you will find a list of sixty-seven items for which to ask forgiveness. According to the classic commentators these sixty-seven items are in fact subject headings for even broader categories which together number many hundreds of actions for which we can ask forgiveness. It's a busy day, to say the least.

The following are but two examples from the vidduy:

1)   *Ashamnu* / **We Have Become Culpable:** this includes, we have acted in ways that deaden our sense of spirituality, we were

driven for profit and thus transgressed G-d's will, we hurt others out of self-centeredness, for our own pleasure we did what we knew was wrong, etc.

2)   ***Al-Chet She-Chatanu Lefanecha B'Emutz HaLev /*** **Hardheartedness:** this includes, refusal to admit that we can be wrong, general stubbornness, denying our shortcomings, lack of compassion for the sick and poor, unwillingness to accept advice, being tough on myself or others when compassion was appropriate, etc.

To say that Yom Kippur is a day for introspection and reflection is true — but it is also an oversimplification. I would like to suggest that you try a little exercise now.

Ask yourself — "How many choices have I been confronted with today?" Mind you, these must be moral choices, choices of import. Not significant life-altering choices, but those small choices which we often pass by, or through, with barely a notice. Examples:

1)   Did you encounter anyone today, a spouse, a child or an acquaintance, whose mood could have been lifted simply by a warm smile or a moment of genuinely expressed concern?

If yes, then ask yourself: (a) what choice did I make at that moment, and (b) how would things have been different, for better or worse, had I chosen otherwise?

2)   How about your attitude in synagogue today. You could use this Yom Kippur as an opportunity for increased self-awareness and personal growth, or you can sit through another year silently bearing the burden of a rather cumbersome experience. Have you considered that choice yet?

3)   Did you have a chance to help someone today? Someone who could have managed without your help but who would have been grateful nonetheless?

Think about how long you had to make that choice. Was it more than a fleeting moment which no one but you will ever know existed?

In retrospect how do you feel about the choice you made? And, do you believe it had a lasting effect on you?

As I know you have realized, these examples are but a drop in the ocean. Everyday we are confronted with tens if not hundreds of little choices. Little, but not so little. Choices that can have either a positive or negative impact on ourselves or someone else.

There are times when we read or hear a concept, and though its meaning may be unclear we have a sense that its profundity demands a closer look. Such a statement is the Torah's assertion that man was created "in the image of G-d." Its meaning is this: man, like G-d, has the capacity to choose. But more, that capacity defines our very essence. We *are* beings who choose.

This being so, it is no wonder that our days and our lives are little more than a continuous string of choices. Most of them small, some not. After all, how often do we choose a career, a spouse or whether or not to have children. These types of choices are few and far between — but there is a vast in-between. A life brimming with choices.

And thus we have Rosh Hashanah and Yom Kippur. The forest and the trees. On Rosh Hashanah we confront the major issues, the general ebb and flow of our lives. On Yom Kippur we dwell on the minutiae. Some would say that Yom Kippur is but a microcosm of Jewish life. A guilt-ridden obsession with trivialities. In fact Yom Kippur is an affirmation of the value of life, of each day and of every aspect of each day. That which we truly cherish is that which we carefully scrutinize. The more significant the whole, the more precious are its details.

Parents are concerned about every aspect of their children's behavior. They know that the sum total of how a child eats his cereal plus how he cares for his belongings, when added to the way he relates to siblings and classmates, eventually adds up to the totality of that child's character. If growth and human development are not to culminate in learning to "eat nicely," then true maturity will lie in taking the reins of the ongoing choices that shape our character.

Senator Dan Coats of Indiana wrote in a recent article, "The only testing ground for the heroic is the mundane. The only preparation for that one profound decision which can change a life, or even a nation, is those hundreds and thousands of half-conscious, self-defining, seemingly insignificant decisions made in private." The sages in the Talmud put it this way: "A person is not given the opportunity for greatness until he is tested in the small things." A Moses or a King David are only entrusted with the destiny of the Jewish people if first they take care that the sheep they tend don't wander off and eat a bit of grass from someone else's field.

Take care. Take care of the small, almost invisible choices. Those precious, precious details of character and life.

In the final analysis there will always exist a symbiotic tension between Rosh Hashanah and Yom Kippur. Rosh Hashanah beckons us to take a panoramic view of our lives, all the while paying scant attention to the nuance that lies therein. Yom Kippur is just the opposite — entirely nuance. The tree, the leaves, and the nourishing roots with barely a thought to the great forest in which we stand.

Only the magnificence of the space shuttle and the unencumbered dreams out of which it grew could make man an ever-frequent visitor to space. Yet all it takes is one overlooked O– Ring — a detail — to bring our dreams crashing down to earth. Or, as someone once observed, "great symphonies begin with just one note."

16

MORNING TORAH READING: SPIRITUALITY AS A RELATIONSHIP

A Thought about Relationships

Thanks to Hollywood's incessant teasing of our own romantic fantasies we often develop a mental and emotional image of who will be the *right one* for me. As a result we find ourselves relating to what we hoped or imagined someone to be, as opposed to who they actually are. In such an instance we are hardly relating at all. Rather we are simply serving our own needs and desires by playing out some predetermined role, thereby ensuring a hollow, lifeless relationship.

Spirituality as a Relationship

The Yom Kippur Torah reading begins by recounting the death of two sons of Aharon, Nadav and Avihu. Elsewhere the Torah relates that these men died because in their unbridled desire to draw closer to G-d they employed an unprescribed procedure in the Temple service.

So what! So they didn't do things exactly as they were told, so they innovated a little bit, is that so terrible? Isn't it true that the only reason they deviated was because they thought this would enhance their spiritual lives and deepen their relationship with G-d?

Tell me if these words sound familiar —

> "... *frankly I consider myself to be a spiritual person...*
> *I really don't need to observe all these commandments*
> *and rituals to be a good Jew or to feel close to G-d ...*
> *I relate to G-d in a way that I feel comfortable with,*
> *and I'm sure that's okay with Him."*

Remember, if you relate to someone in terms of who you want them to be instead of who they are or by means that feel "right" to you but are inappropriate for them, then in truth you have no relationship at all (regardless of how good it may feel). In the dimension of spirituality, of relating to G-d, the same holds true.

More to Sacrifices Than Meets the Eye

During the periods when the Temple stood in Jerusalem the central focus of Jewish life was an elaborate system of communal and personal sacrifices and offerings. How is this possible? Aren't priestly orders and sacrificial rites the domain of primitive peoples bearing an elementary view of the world and how to relate to it?

Surely the Jewish people, a people endowed with insights a millennia ahead of their time, a people who repeatedly espoused ideas and values that were at odds with the prevailing mood, should have easily seen beyond these crude, barbaric practices. And what's more, how do we deal with rational, sophisticated modern Jews who to this day mourn the loss of the Temple and its sacrificial service?

Are sacrifices a disturbing historical anomaly better glossed over than scrutinized — a sort of intellectual scandal in an otherwise brilliant career — or is there some way that we can begin to make sense of that which indeed occupies perhaps a fifth of all the teachings in the Torah?

To Draw Close

In Hebrew the term for sacrifice — *korban* — literally means *to draw close*. The Jewish people always understood that G-d lacks nothing and therefore has no needs. Sacrifices are not *for* G-d, nor are they meant to appease Him or cajole Him to act in one way or another. The primary function of the sacrifice is to affect us in such a way as to enable us to enhance our relationship with G-d.

We have already pointed out that for genuine closeness to develop in a relationship you must understand and be sensitive to the one you are relating to. The flip side is that you must also possess a sufficient measure of self-awareness so that in fact it is *you* — and not some socially imposed portrait of yourself — who is involved in the relationship. And true, while we can never fully know ourselves, still, the greater our level of self-knowledge the deeper and richer will be our contribution to the relationship. The sacrifice then, in fact the entire Temple service was a stage teeming with images which served to edify our knowledge of ourselves and how to draw closer to G-d.

Here are two examples from the Yom Kippur Torah reading regarding various aspects of the Temple service and how they served as educational tools to elevate man's character and refine his spirit so that he could draw ever closer to the transcendental source of all existence.

1)   Verses 16:7–10. *"Then he shall take the two he-goats . . ."*

Listen carefully to the detail of observance at work in this "sacrifice."

Two identical goats. Identical in size, appearance and value. Both are standing in a similar manner at the threshold of the sanctuary. Both have a perfectly balanced opportunity to be used positively in the Temple or to be cast away and destroyed.

Is there a more poignant message for Yom Kippur? Free will, our freedom to choose our path, our actions and our destiny. We are stubborn goats, yes, but stubborn goats with a choice. Do we use our iron will to maintain our integrity and commitment to morality and G-d or do we use that same will to shield ourselves from infusing our lives with a G-dly dimension.

We are besieged by a host of forces, psychological and others, which lay claim to our free-willed ability to make life's most monumental choices. On Yom Kippur the eyes of the Jew are riveted on an image that proclaims our freedom. In life we must know that the power and responsibility to choose lies firmly in our hands.

2)   Verse 16:14 *"Then he will take from blood of the bullock... and in front of the covering he shall sprinkle seven times from the blood of his finger."*

The ceremony of sprinkling the blood seven times in a downward motion also included an eighth sprinkling in an upward fashion. The world was created in seven days and thus the number seven represents the physical world and life as it is lived on a daily basis. The number eight goes one step beyond and represents that which is transcendent. This is why the *bris mila*, the covenant between man (this world) and G-d (transcendence), takes place on the eighth day.

I know of someone who went to India to study in an ashram for a number of years. On a return visit to Chicago he was riding a bus when he became aware of something that shook him to his very core. He realized that he looked down on the people around him — ants, he thought to himself, mere unenlightened ants. He realized, "after all the lofty experiences, and after all I've learned and imbibed, if this is how I look at human beings then what have I really gained?"

The *kohen* — the priest — would first execute one sprinkle upwards followed by seven downwards. Our first inclinations must be directed towards that which transcends the superficial mundanity of this world, but beware, if our spiritual lives and experiences are not translated into how we live on a daily basis — in the here and now — then it is spirituality corrupted. Yes, Yom Kippur is a day imbued with lofty potential, but it is a potential that must express itself in the weeks and months that ensue.

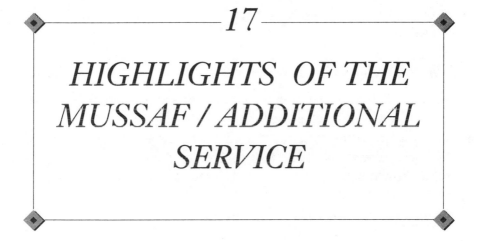

17

HIGHLIGHTS OF THE MUSSAF / ADDITIONAL SERVICE

The Service of the Kohen Gadol / **The High Priest**

Michael Jordan, Lee Iacocca and Jane Fonda. Each an icon in their own right. A symbol of "what makes this country great" and a model for what any kid in America can grow up to be.

You can tell a lot about a person — or a people — by those they look up to. The *Kohen Gadol* was not merely a religious functionary — he was a model of the nation's ideals. He bore the awesome burden of striving in every way to approximate the most virtuous traits of character towards which all Jews must endeavor.

V'at Zehavim / **He Wore Golden Garments**

The *Kohen Gadol* wore eight garments. Each garment represented a fundamental aspect of human character which he was reminded to be particularly attuned to.

Whenever there is an election there inevitably arises those "test of character" issues. Where were you during the war, where were you during Woodstock, where were you when your wife wasn't looking, and so forth.

For Jewish leadership, and really for each of us, character is everything.

U'paro Mutzav / His Ox Stood between the Chamber & Altar

Life is a field to be plowed. Deeds are seeds to be planted and the development of character is a bounty to be harvested. The ox takes one plodding step after another until finally the job is done. And so it is with us — one foot in front of the other — there is no telling how much we can eventually accomplish.

Achas V'Sheva / One and Seven

One sprinkling went upwards while seven went down towards the ground. While the *Kohen Gadol* was immersed in the most lofty of spiritual endeavors, he always had to remain in touch with the realities of daily life.

They say you can tell the righteousness of a man by the smile on the face of his wife.

Ani U'Vaisi / I and My Family

On Yom Kippur the *Kohen Gadol* would enter the Holy of Holies (the inner sanctum of the Temple) as a representative of the entire Jewish people. At the same time however, the Temple service demanded that he not forget his responsibilities to his own family.

You know of course that it is easier to love humanity than to go out of your way to help your next door neighbor. A lot of people drive around with bumper stickers proclaiming — *Let's Bring Peace to the World* — or — *Mankind: Together We Can Make a Difference*. Do you ever wonder what their family lives are like?

Shigro B'Yad Ish Iti / Into the Hand of the Appointed Man

The expression for *"appointed man"* is an unusual one and also carries the connotation — *"the timeless man."*

Fashions and fads come and go. Be they clothing, diets or the latest therapy. But what about values? Are they, too, nothing but vulnerable prey for the shifting winds of societal mood?

Timeless man calls out to us — he challenges us. Raise your sights above the din of popular opinion. Brave the storm. And stand for something — now — and forever.

The Ten Martyrs

Ayleh Ezkerah / These I Will Remember

In the words of Mark Twain, *"The Egyptian, the Babylonian and the Persian rose, filled the planet with sound and splendor, then faded to dream stuff and passed away; the Greek and the Roman followed, and made a vast noise, and they are gone . . . All things are mortal but the Jew; all other forces pass, but he remains."* And what about the French, the British and the Americans. How long until they too are relegated to the quiet halls of museum exhibitions visited only by curious strangers — and by Jews.

True, *Am Yisroel Chai*, the Jewish people live. And so do Rabbi Yishmael, Rabbi Akiva and the other martyrs. Their words have guided and inspired us for all of these centuries. But what's more, we still talk to them. Everyday countless students of the Talmud, of Jewish thought and wisdom, study their words in schools and yeshivot all over the world. Their words are alive! Seriously reckoned with and hotly debated. We live because they live. But if they pass — what will become of us?

Ki Anu Amecha / For We Are Your People

This prayer is usually sung by the congregation together with the chazzan (cantor). In truth, it is a love song. Each verse expresses another facet of the relationship between G-d and the Jewish people.

Wherever there is depth in a relationship there is also endless nuance and subtlety. Each depicting another dimension of a much greater and deeper totality.

18

AFTERNOON TORAH READING: THE FINE ART OF SELF-CONTROL

In his magnum opus, Maimonides codified all of Jewish life and practice into fourteen volumes. One of these volumes is entitled *The Book of Holiness*. The curious thing about this book is that it contains nothing that seems to be of a particularly holy nature. It doesn't deal with prayer, with loving G-d, with the observances in the Temple or anything else that one might conventionally consider to be holy.

The Book of Holiness addresses two general areas of Jewish law. One is that of forbidden foods and the other is forbidden sexual relations. So what does not eating a cheeseburger or not having incestual relations have to do with holiness? The answer is plain — in Judaism holiness means to be the master of your physical desires. In no way do we more resemble animals than in our desire to fulfill our bodily appetites. Of one thing you can be sure — there is no such thing as an animal with self-control. They just don't diet — ever!

Human beings have a choice. We can control our desires or they will certainly control us. The choice of self-mastery is the choice to be human. It is also the foundation of sanctity.

The Torah reading for Yom Kippur afternoon deals with the issue of controlling our most basic appetites. We can fast, we can pray — we can read the prayer book from cover to cover and pound our hearts for an entire day — but it is our ability to control and direct our desires — not to quash them — that will ultimately determine the tenor of our character.

The Haftorah of Yonah

". . . and they called for a fast and they donned sackcloth, from the greatest amongst them to the smallest . . . and G-d saw their actions . . . and G-d relented . . ."

The people of Nineveh wore sackcloth, fasted, and poured their hearts out in prayer. And G-d responded. Not to their sackcloth, not to their fasting and prayers, but to their *"actions."*

G-d saw that their actions had changed. Isn't it obvious that this is what really counts? Our actions, our deeds, the way we live.

On Yom Kippur we deny certain pleasures to our body, to the animal aspect of our nature. We don't eat and we don't engage in sexual relations. Likewise we don't bathe, wear comfortable leather shoes, or anoint ourselves with any oils, perfumes, or lotions.

By taking a day off, by taking a step back from our bodily interests, we move two steps closer to the key to personal growth. When you step back from a situation you can gain a fresh perspective and regain control of that situation, of yourself and of life.

We are our actions. And, we have the ability to change. Beneath it all Yom Kippur is an expression of confidence in our ability to take control of our lives.

Shepherds come in all shapes and sizes — as do sheep. To lead or to follow. Yom Kippur challenges us. The choice is ours — to assert control over our own lives or to capitulate to every fragrant aroma and fanciful whim that comes our way.

19

NEILAH: THE CLOSING MOMENTS

Neilah is a time of contrary emotions. Exhaustion and elation walk hand in hand. If you have tried to realize the potential for growth inherent in every moment of Yom Kippur then there is a part of you that must surely be drained. But you can't stop yet, not when the summit is so close. It's now time to draw on your second wind. This is the Super Bowl, and overtime is about to begin.

In Jerusalem, everyone has a story. This is about a lovely man named Chaim.

At the age of 86, Chaim decided that it was time he began to learn a little about his religion — Judaism. Together with his wife, who was 85, they took leave of their comfortable home in San Diego and headed, in his words, *"right for the source"* — Jerusalem.

These two enthusiasts spent an enchanted summer in the restored Jewish Quarter of the Old City of Jerusalem. They chose a program of study specifically designed for adults with little or no background in Jewish studies. With their arrival, the average age of the participants in this program immediately jumped by about 45 years. The entire group adopted them as grandparents.

Time passed quickly and soon these two jewels were safely back home in San Diego. Ten months later — they were back.

One afternoon Chaim and I were walking together to the *Kotel* — the Western Wall. I asked him this question: "Chaim, how is it that at 86 you suddenly had a desire to come and study Torah in Israel? What happened?"

This is the story he told me:

> "*I grew up in Russia and though we were proud of being Jewish, my family was not very religious. At a young age manhood was thrust upon me and I was suddenly a soldier in the Russian army.*
>
> *I knew that the holidays were approaching but I didn't know exactly when. Rosh Hashanah came and went before I found out that Yom Kippur was only a few days off. I decided that I would fast. And you should know, this was dangerous and strictly forbidden in the army. As it was there were days with little or no rations. Nonetheless, I had resolved to fast.*
>
> *So there I was on Yom Kippur — mile after bitterly cold mile. Marching and fasting, marching and fasting, when all at once it occurred to me. If it was Yom Kippur and if I was fasting then shouldn't I also be praying. So I resolved to pray. There was one problem though — I didn't know how.*
>
> *I searched my mind until I came upon the only Hebrew words I knew: **avadim hayinu lepharoh b'mitzrayim** — "we were slaves to Pharaoh in Egypt." You see, one thing my family did observe was the Passover Seder, and for some reason those words from the haggadah stayed with me.*
>
> *These words became my Yom Kippur prayers. **Avadim hayinu lepharoh b'mitzrayim** — "we were slaves to Pharaoh in Egypt." Over and over I repeated those words. A thousand times if not more. Marching and praying, marching and praying."*
>
> *We were now standing in the shadow of the Kotel — "Somehow, somehow," he concluded, "I know that I am here today because of that Yom Kippur prayer."*

Neilah. The starry night is closing in around us. The majestic opportunity of Yom Kippur — the gates are about to close.

Chaim is our teacher now. Do you hear his message?

Our prayers? Somehow it's not the words that matter — as long as you mean it, like he did. Somehow those words, that Passover passage transposed to a Yom Kippur prayer, became etched in a reality that stood by Chaim for a lifetime. Finally, at the right moment, they led him by the hand to Jerusalem.

Neilah. Just one word. One heartfelt prayer. In the end — now — that is all it will take.

I would suggest that at this time, you take a few minutes to review your day. What are the one or two most important things you wanted to accomplish today? When during the day did you feel most "tuned in" to what Yom Kippur was all about — when were you most moved? At what point did you feel most in touch with yourself or closest to G-d? Focus on those goals and moments, those feelings and insights.

As you begin *Neilah* ask yourself — if I could accomplish only one step of growth today, what would that step be? *Neilah* is the time to make sure that if you achieve nothing else — though you surely will — that at least that one step of growth will now become a lasting part of who you are. Who you will forever be.

Elokei Avraham . . . / G-d of Abraham, G-d of Isaac . . .

Where do I belong? Where do I fit in? Where do I even begin?

The G-d of Abraham, the G-d of Isaac, the G-d of Jacob. Each one had to discover who he was. As do we. Each had to become the master craftsman of his own sense of self, and with that, to fashion a novel form of relating to G-d.

Each possessed a singular soul and destiny. Each had a unique contribution to make. To the Jewish people and to history.

It seems so very difficult. But this is what life — and Yom Kippur — are all about. Our forefathers set the pace. All we need is the courage to follow.

V'Chasmeynu B'Sefer Ha-Chaim / Seal Us in the Book of Life

Judgment is a reflection of our choices and commitments.

Have you ever assured someone with the words, *"consider it done."* If those words mean anything then they mean the following: "I just want you to know that with regards to the particular action we are discussing — no matter what obstacles arise — the job *will* be done. As a matter of fact, it is as good as done right now."

With mettled spirits we now seal our efforts and our prayers — "consider it done."

Siym Shalom / Grant Peace . . . to All of Israel Your People

Sometimes it seems that if it weren't for the issues that divide us there would be nothing left to bind us together. What a bitter irony. Periodically however, we are reminded of the truth. That all we have is one another.

The events that made up the opening rounds of the Six Day War are legendary. But what was life like just one day before the war began?

If you don't remember, speak to those who do. All over the world Jews feared what few dared to utter. The unthinkable — Israel would fall. A furious torrent of blood would bathe the streets of Jerusalem, Tel Aviv, and Haifa.

A s the war began, thousands of Jews huddled together in bomb shelters all across Israel. No one knew what would be. Was this the end the Arabs had promised?

In one such shelter was Rabbi Chaim Shmulevitz. He was one of Jerusalem's great sages. A man who together with his yeshiva had escaped Europe and spent the war years in Shanghai — studying and teaching Torah to those who had escaped with him. In Jerusalem his wise counsel was sought by young and old — religious and secular.

There in the shelter together with Rabbi Shmulevitz and all the rest was a woman who seemed to be alone. Her husband had abandoned her many years before. One day he just vanished, leaving her with five young children to raise, bills to pay, and no means of income. Her heart was forever shattered.

There they were deep within the earth. Would this be a shelter or would it be a grave? Her tired eyes looked heavenward.

*"**Ribbono shel olam** — Master of the World, years ago my husband left me in a broken condition. What I have toiled to build has been a bitter fate — my life. Master of the World, I want you to know that I have forgiven that man with all my heart. I bear no grudge or hatred. Master of the World, if I can forgive him then surely you can forgive your children — the Jewish people."*

At that moment, said Rabbi Chaim Shmulevitz, the safety of the Jewish nation had been guaranteed. With that prayer the clouds of war would pass.

As Yom Kippur fades away it is time to consider another commitment. Our commitment to our fellow Jews. What if we make this a year when Jews are concerned about and actively committed to one another's well-being without there being a crisis? No hostages, no tragedies, no gas masks.

It's possible, you know.

Ata Notyn Yad / **You Extend a Hand**

As a wise man once said — *"It ain't over till it's over."*

Everyday is a lifetime. Young and vital — singing a song of the renewal of life's potential.

G-d's hand is outstretched. No matter where we are today, if we make a true effort to be where we know we should be tomorrow — we will succeed. The stunning power of free will is that we are not prisoners of our past. And as for our future — if you knew G-d would help, is there anything you couldn't do?

Elokai, N'tzor Leshoni / G-d, Guard My Tongue from Evil

Some people are highly skilled at the use of firearms. If they wanted they could kill. Yet others know how to use their bare hands. Swift and deadly movements — they too can kill.

If you say the right words to a person — or more precisely — if you say the wrong words, you too can kill. This requires no special training. Likewise, the right words, said in the right way, can give a person new hope. A refreshed spirit. A new lease on life. This too we can all accomplish.

If we take our words seriously then we will take life seriously. We conclude Neilah and Yom Kippur as we conclude every prayer service. Knowing that one word can make all the difference in the world.

20

EPILOGUE: THE MORNING AFTER

On the day following Yom Kippur there are some synagogues that have a custom to begin the morning services fifteen minutes early. This custom is clearly meant to demonstrate that we have changed. We are not prepared to step back into the same rut we were in before the holidays. After all the efforts of Rosh Hashanah and Yom Kippur our approach to life is fresh and vital. Our vigor and idealism are renewed. Things *will* be different.

A friend once related another perspective on this custom of rising early after Yom Kippur. "If you live your life differently, for even fifteen minutes" he said, "then it was all worthwhile."

The legendary Rabbi Yisroel Salanter is said to have observed that "it is easier to master the entire Talmud than to improve just one aspect of your character." To the Jewish way of thinking, life is about growth, and every step of growth is a diamond to be treasured.

If in some way this book has helped you to use Rosh Hashanah and Yom Kippur as opportunities for growth, then we have achieved a lot. If you now possess an enhanced appreciation of the value inherent in Jewish life, then I would ask you, please — share it with a friend. For their benefit, for ours, and for the Jewish people.

FUTURE PUBLICATIONS

© *The Passover Survival Kit.*
   Publication Date: December 1992.

© *The Jewish Marriage Survival Kit.*
   Publication Date: June 1993.

◇ **HOW TO ORDER** ◇

Retail: The *Rosh Hashanah Yom Kippur Survival Kit* is $8.50 plus postage and handling.

A Unique Gift Idea

This year, send more than a card, send the gift of wisdom.

1-800-860-0774
Large order discounts available.

Wholesale: Schools, synagogues and community organizations can use the *Rosh Hashanah Yom Kippur Survival Kit* for educational, PR and fundraising purposes. Discount group rates of over 70% off retail are available for special orders.

To Order: Call 1-800-860-0774. Outside the U.S. call (614) 338-0774 or write to Leviathan Press Marketing, 66 North Merkle Rd., P.O. Box 43209-0448, Columbus, Ohio 43209.